THE WHITE DEVIL AND THE DUCHESS OF MALFI

Text and Performance

RICHARD ALLEN CAVE

MACMILLAN EDUCATION

First published 1988

Published by
MACMILLAN EDUCATION LTD
Houndmills, Basingstoke, Hampshire RG21 2XS
and London
Companies and representatives
throughout the world

Typeset by Wessex Typesetters
(Division of The Eastern Press Ltd)
Frome, Somerset

Printed in Hong Kong

British Library Cataloguing in Publication Data
Cave, Richard Allen
The white devil and The Duchess of Malfi.
——(Text and performance).
1. Webster, John, *1580?–1625?*. Duchess of
Malfi   2. Webster, John, *1580?–1625?*
White devil
I. Title   II. Series
822'.3   PR3184.D83
ISBN 0–333–39577–8

CONTENTS

Illustrations will be found in Part Two

ACKNOWLEDGEMENTS

Quotations from the texts of the tragedies are taken from David Gunby's edition of *John Webster: Three Plays*, published in the Penguin English Library (Harmondsworth, 1972). All critical material relating to Webster cited in the following study is listed in the Bibliography.

All scholars working seriously on Webster's plays must admit a debt to John Russell Brown's superb editions of the tragedies for The Revels Plays series published by Methuen (*The White Devil*, 1960; *The Duchess of Malfi*, 1964).

I am grateful to Professor Inga-Stina Ewbank and Dr J. S. Bratton, with whom over many years I have discussed aspects of Webster's drama in the course of teaching Renaissance theatre and to the many students in tutorial, seminar and workshop who have enhanced my understanding of the plays in performance. My sincere thanks are also due to Enid Foster and her staff at the library of the British Theatre Association; to Dr Marian Pringle of the Shakespeare Centre, Stratford-upon-Avon; to the staff of both the Scripts and the Press and Publicity departments at the National Theatre, London; to Edward Bond and Margaret Ramsay for permission to study his acting version of *The White Devil*; to Zoe Dominic, John Vere Brown and John Haynes for permission to use their photographs of the productions studied in Part Two and for their help in locating pictures that capture the essential qualities of these stagings most graphically; to Mrs Brenda Townend, who typed portions of the manuscript; and above all to my wife who assisted at every stage of the venture with tireless energy.

I would like to dedicate this book to Eric Swift who first encouraged my studies of Renaissance theatre and took a gauche sixth-former on a memorable expedition to see Peggy Ashcroft in *The Duchess of Malfi* at Stratford in 1960.

GENERAL EDITOR'S PREFACE

For many years a mutual suspicion existed between the theatre director and the literary critic of drama. Although in the first half of the century there were important exceptions, such was the rule. A radical change of attitude, however, has taken place over the last thirty years. Critics and directors now increasingly recognise the significance of each other's work and acknowledge their growing awareness of interdependence. Both interpret the same text, but do so according to their different situations and functions. Without the director, the designer and the actor, a play's existence is only partial. They revitalise the text with action, enabling the drama to live fully at each performance. The academic critic investigates the script to elucidate its textual problems, understand its conventions and discover how it operates. He may also propose his view of the work, expounding what he considers to be its significance.

Dramatic texts belong therefore to theatre and to literature. The aim of the 'Text and Performance' series is to achieve a fuller recognition of how both enhance our enjoyment of the play. Each volume follows the same basic pattern. Part One provides a critical introduction to the play under discussion, using the techniques and criteria of the literary critic in examining the manner in which the work operates through language, imagery and action. Part Two takes the enquiry further into the play's theatricality by focusing on selected productions of recent times so as to illustrate points of contrast and comparison in the interpretation of different directors and actors, and to demonstrate how the drama has worked on the modern stage. In this way the series seeks to provide a lively and informative introduction to major plays in their text and performance.

Michael Scott

PLOT SYNOPSES AND SOURCES

The White Devil

The Duke of Brachiano becomes infatuated with Vittoria Corombona, the wife of Camillo, and seduces her with the aid of his secretary, Flamineo, Vittoria's brother. She instructs the Duke through a cleverly devised account of a dream to murder his wife and her husband. Brachiano privately divorces Isabella, his wife, and has her poisoned; Flamineo organises the death of Camillo. But Isabella was sister to Francisco de Medici, Duke of Florence, and Camillo nephew to Cardinal Monticelso and the murders bring the lovers powerful enemies in State and Church. Vittoria is arrested and tried for adultery and murder; the trial is a travesty of justice; her judges (Monticelso and Francisco) can make no real case against her but they have her imprisoned in a House of Convertites, thus publicly branding her a whore. Francisco decides to pursue his revenge in private and suborns Lodovico, a notorious murderer, to assist him; he then skilfully contrives to get Vittoria abducted from prison by Brachiano, who takes her to his palace at Padua and marries her. Francisco follows them disguised as a Moor, Mulinassar. During the tournament to celebrate the wedding, Francisco and his henchmen poison Brachiano's helmet and subsequently strangle him. Flamineo, enraged at failing to gain preferment by the marriage, first kills his brother Marcello, then persuades Vittoria to join him in a suicide pact. She shoots him and tramples on his body only to discover he has tricked her (the pistols were not loaded) to test her strength of purpose. The two are trapped by Lodovico; he puts them to a lingering death before he is himself slain by command of Brachiano's young heir.

Sources

These are chiefly historical, events recorded in the play taking place in Italy in the years 1576–85. While many printed accounts of the lives of Vittoria and Brachiano exist, none can be specifically designated Webster's actual source.

The Duchess of Malfi

The widowed Duchess of Malfi privately courts her young steward, Antonio, a man whose impeccable nature she has long admired. They wed secretly despite the fact that she has repeatedly been warned against a second marriage by her brothers, the Cardinal and Ferdinand, Duke of Calabria, who talk of not dishonouring their Aragonian blood but who desire to inherit her property. Ferdinand is incestuously attracted to his sister and plants a spy, Bosola, in her entourage to report on her behaviour. For some years the lovers contrive to keep their marriage a secret despite rumours which are current when the Duchess conceives and gives birth to a child. Bosola discovers that the Duchess is wed but cannot determine the identity of her husband. Ferdinand visits the Duchess by night, hoping to trap the unknown husband in her room but, failing to do so, he savagely condemns his sister for her 'looseness' and vows never to see her again. Panic-struck the Duchess and Antonio plan to flee to Ancona and in a thoughtless moment the Duchess confides to the kindly-seeming Bosola who her husband is. The couple are publicly shamed at Ancona by the Cardinal; they part for Antonio's better safety. The Duchess is captured by Bosola and Ferdinand; she is subjected to a series of hideous tortures in the hope of reducing her to abject despair and is finally strangled. Ferdinand grows insane with remorse; the repentant Bosola decides to join with Antonio but, mistaking him for the Cardinal, kills him. Overwhelmed with anguish, Bosola stabs both the Aragonian brothers but himself receives a fatal wound from Ferdinand.

Sources

Again historical, relating to events that took place between 1505 and 1513. But Webster clearly knew of them through one or more of the many fictional accounts popular in the early seventeenth century; Painter's *The Palace of Pleasure* (1566–67) is considered the most likely influence.

PART ONE: TEXT

1 INTRODUCTION

Webster has never lacked critical detractors since his first audience for *The White Devil* at the Red Bull in Clerkenwell. What is remarkable is how repetitive the criticisms are: that he is 'a master of scenes rather than structure', a view (first voiced by John Wilson in 1818) which, it is claimed, Webster's confession of being a slow worker somehow supports; that he had 'a wild and undigested' genius (Theobald, 1733) which is often a polite way of saying he was a sensation-monger emulating Madame Tussaud and her chamber of horrors (G. H. Lewes, 1850 and Shaw); that his plays show the want of a developed moral sense, since being 'much possessed by death' (T. S. Eliot, 1920) he was clearly the victim of his own morbidity. All lines of attack question Webster's artistic integrity and suggest a fundamental unease with his work: Shakespeare – invariably the detractors' yardstick – is *healthier* by comparison. There is a risk any dramatist courts who chooses to explore the roots of violence in the human psyche: that he will be judged a purveyor rather than a portrayer of decadence, a man imaginatively obsessed rather than critically detached. (Edward Bond is such a figure in our own time.)

Webster has had his champions: Charles Lamb (1808) saw a decorum in the horrors because the dramatist's aim was through them 'to touch a soul to the quick'; Swinburne (1886) praised the scruple and discrimination with which Webster stayed the right side of that 'delicate line' which 'divides the impressive and the terrible from the horrible and the loathsome'; literary historians like F. L. Lucas (1927) have argued that his capricious and inconsistent stagecraft has to be accepted as 'the fashion of the day'. Such defences often seem like special pleading, since none fundamentally challenges the view that Webster is a designer of loosely connected 'big' scenes. What is needed is a demonstration of how a highly-tuned moral imagination is shaping each tragedy into a unified whole. Interestingly Lucas undermines his argument by observing that '*The White Devil*, well acted, can carry an audience breathless with it over all the breaks and rough places in its plot'. If *in the theatre* the effect is of an 'irresistible onrush', can the plot properly be described as having 'breaks' and 'rough places'? That Webster's is a wholly theatrical art best understood in terms of performance has been the critical trend since the late fifties; this argues that he consciously exploits the very nature of theatre with its focus on *acting* to explore the impulses that control human behaviour regardless of an individual's stated beliefs or purpose. The multiform but always urgent and wayward nature of passion is what in the modern view excites Webster's tragic awareness and imaginative sympathy: the sheer difficulty of being true to self which, far from inducing apathy, seems to compel his characters to live at a pitch of intensity. Noticeably in his 'To the Reader' in the Quarto of *The White Devil* Webster dismissed the coarse responses of the Red Bull audience because what they wanted was only that intensity and sensationalism. The 'full and understanding auditory' he appealed to must reach beyond that to appreciate the metaphysical dimension that the plays inhabit which forms a ground swell to the action, surfacing poignantly in the characters' sudden consuming anguish.

2 WEBSTER'S POETRY AS DRAMATIC VERSE

A study of Webster's theatre art should perhaps begin with the poetry where, for critics making comparisons with Shakespeare, he comes off worse, since it but rarely achieves a sustained lyricism. While metaphors abound they are used fitfully, discarded once their immediate effect has registered; they are not treated developmentally as by Shakespeare who makes the transformations and patterning of imagery organic to his purpose, a means of illuminating the inner thematic debate of his plays. Metaphor is frequently Shakespeare's means of intimating that *other* dimension. Webster's verbal artistry is very different, its richness largely dependent on the fact of performance: dramatic context affords a wealth of allusion.

To judge by his writing on the subject, sententiousness was what Webster prized, the shaping of experience into proverbial, moral or philosophical axioms (*sententiae*). This sounds aridly cerebral, and there is a danger of misconception here. It is known that Webster borrowed copiously from popular contemporary texts and translations; talk of his reliance on Renaissance commonplaces suggests the trite and, where verse couplets are concerned, doggerel. *Heard* in context, the effect is often of a character's seeking comfort and security in proverbial wisdom which the audience with its greater awareness of the play's action knows to be cruel illusion. At its simplest, the use affords a powerful dramatic irony. But the device can be taken further. Consider Antonio's observation to the Duchess [III v 72] in the scene following their banishment from Ancona and after receipt of Ferdinand's ominous letter: '*Man, like to cassia, is prov'd best being bruis'd*'. It is a hollow comfort he offers his wife and she quickly retorts: 'Must I like to a slave-born Russian / Account it `praise to suffer tyranny?'. Adversity highlights a crucial difference of temperament in the couple. She is patrician, with an aristocrat's fearlessness of threat; homeless, deprived of retinue, she is Duchess of Malfi still in the core of her being – a quality that subsequent experience is to refine into spiritual strength. He, for all the honour she gives him, remains a commoner at heart, submissive before displays of power. How ironic and prophetic now seem the words he uttered when the Duchess in wooing him calmed (by force of personality) his fears of reprisal from her brothers: 'These words should be mine' [I ii 390]. Except in their one scene of sexual intimacy [III ii 1–57], hers is always the decisive voice, alert to circumstance; his is dependent, quick to succumb to apprehension, his love, courage, honour having their limits. Departing from her for, as they suppose, his better safety, his whole consciousness is numbed with dread: 'My heart is turn'd to a heavy lump of lead, / With which I sound my danger' [III v 88–9]. The *sententia* here sharpens our sense of character and for an alert audience resonates with meanings beyond the stated.

A couplet from *The White Devil* is often cited out of context as a succinct summary of Webster's moral philosophy:

> Glories, like glow-worms, afar off shine bright
> But look'd to near, have neither heat nor light
> [v i 41–2]

This affords an ironic comment on the play's action, but that is only part of its effect. Flamineo is excitedly singing the praises of one Mulinassar, a Moor, recently arrived at Brachiano's court, one who like himself delights in expressing a 'deep contempt / Of our slight airy courtiers' [*ll*. 36–7]. The couplet is a reflection not of Flamineo's but the Moor's attitudes and manner to which Flamineo acquiesces: he has found his match in malcontented railing; hence his glee. Immediately after the *sententia* a procession enters headed by Brachiano with the Moor, and Flamineo breaks off his talk to Hortensio with the exclamation: 'The Duke!'. He refers to Brachiano; but the audience is shocked to perceive that Mulinassar is the disguised Duke of Florence. Francisco has been growing into the play's most cunning Machiavel; from this point on, the action follows a pattern largely under his control, and, though the characters think themselves free agents, they are actors in a scenario of his devising. Throughout Act IV we watch Francisco becoming a consummate actor himself, tricking Monticelso over the 'black book' [IV i], composing an ardent love-letter to Vittoria to provoke Brachiano's jealousy, feigning horror before his servant at the news of her escape from the House of Convertites, for which he schemed, and duping Lodovico into complicity with his pursuit of revenge. Flamineo is dangerous; it is essential that Francisco relax his enemy's guard and clearly he has done this by assuming Flamineo's own ranting, satirical vein, striking up a seeming concord that gives his victim a false sense of security. Webster might have dramatised their encounter; instead in a brilliantly succinct feat of exposition, he gives us Flamineo's elation and immediately undermines it with an ominous stage-picture. Francisco is one 'glow-worm' who will give 'neither heat nor light'. Flamineo's reckless excitability (soon to take a lethal turn) and Francisco's power, resource and nerve are graphically delineated. Always as the characters reach for the assurance and command over experience implicit in *sententiae* the stage-action exposes the limits of their perception and their painful vulnerability. There is nothing capricious about such artistry.

The juxtaposition of verbal and visual effects often endows the language with an intricacy of reference which is poetic but not necessarily metaphorical. When, for example, Brachiano insists Flamineo seek pardon nightly for Marcello's death, Flamineo retorts 'Your will is law now, I'll not meddle with it' [v ii 78]. He means he will not contest Brachiano's authority; but 'will' to the Elizabethans signified both 'command' and 'sexual appetite' for which, as Brachiano's pander to Vittoria, Flamineo has 'meddled' in earnest at the cost of Isabella and Camillo's lives. Even as he speaks, the audience sees Lodovico poison Brachiano's helmet, 'meddling' for revenge occasioned by the Duke's lust and in a manner that will soon silence Brachiano's power ('will') for ever. Then there are occasions when images acquire symbolic overtones by repeated verbal and visual illustration. Brachiano ends his marriage to Isabella by a ritual that reverses the pattern of the nuptial service concluding with a refusal to kiss her ever again. By a cruel logic her murder, seen in dumbshow, involves Isabella's kissing her husband's portrait, the lips of which are poisoned; and their son agonises that he is as a consequence denied the right to pay his last proper respects to her by kissing her dead mouth. Even to the child's innocent mind, a decorum, a piety has been grossly abused, though he can express his feeling only tentatively – but poignantly – through the memory of how she suckled him as a baby, 'And it should seem by that she dearly lov'd me / Since princes seldom do it' [III ii 334–5]. Brachiano dies, his face disfigured by poison, refusing to let Vittoria kiss him lest she suffer too [v iii 27]. It is a magnanimous gesture (in his crisis of pain, his thought is of her not himself and that is a token of love) but there is an inexorable logic and poetic necessity in his action. He began the play vowing to Vittoria – 'you shall to me at once / Be dukedom, health, wife, children, friends and all' [I ii 265–6]; and she has cost him everything. In retrospect there is a bitter irony in the first words he utters when, seeing Vittoria, he confesses his infatuation to Flamineo: 'Quite lost' [I ii 3]. Dying, he does not rail against her as the occasion of his downfall, he accepts his fate but that fate denies him the fitting expression of his feelings – a kiss – which might solace his end. It is this patterning of verbal and visual images that makes Brachiano's death more than sensational.

Given the density of implication that accrues to language in the tragedies making for subtle networks of relations between scenes and speeches, an audience from the first must be made alert to how characters use language, since in many cases the characters' voyage into self-awareness involves the discovery that there is more in what they say than they initially supposed. Both plays open with scenes that invite an audience to be intently sensitive to tone and begin imaginatively to hear a subtext. *The White Devil* pitches us headlong into a scene that is morally bewildering. The banished Lodovico curses his fate. Yet from his companions' account of his life his sentence seems lenient: he has squandered a fortune in riotous living and committed 'certain murders' apparently as Brachiano's confederate. As an aristocrat Lodovico's power was near-absolute but, financially ruined, he is no longer so free an agent and it riles him to submit to the conditions governing common men's existence. His fury is the mark of a patrician sensibility that believed itself *above* petty considerations like justice; under sentence, he rails at the *injustice* of any moral law that would seek to restrain his will. Antonelli urges 'Have a full man within you' [I i 44] – that is, be sufficient to yourself, cultivate equanimity. Lodovico is derisive: 'Leave your painted comforts' [*l.* 50]; having been a 'full man' on his own terms, he sees this as adding insult to injury. It goads him to threaten violence on his enemies: 'I'll make Italian cut-works in their guts / If ever I return' [*ll.* 51–2]. Left alone, he curtly defines his lot:

> Great men sell sheep, thus to be cut to pieces,
> When first they have shorn them bare and sold their fleeces.
>
> [*ll.* 61–2]

Lodovico rages in self-pity at his new-found impotence: extravagance and violence were his habitual modes of expressing his wealth and position; impoverished and an outcast, he can no longer be himself. This is forceful exposition. It presents us with a dangerous individual so destitute of moral scruple and self-awareness that, later in the play, he can easily be manipulated by Francisco as a tool to effect the final carnage. More importantly the scene renders vividly for us the nature of one kind of patrician mind that sees itself as standing outside conventional behaviour by virtue of rank. Brachiano and Francisco similarly act in the belief that the aristocratic will is law unto itself. Introduced first to Lodovico whose consciousness is distraught at losing the freedoms he has been conditioned to consider his innate right, we can the better appreciate and judge Brachiano and Francisco: their complete assurance, their self-possession are rooted, we discover, in utter shamelessness. Knowing Lodovico's mind we can more easily penetrate behind their ease of manner. Lodovico's railing against fate enables us in time too to discriminate Flamineo's differently pitched tirades against world, fortune, status, family, as occasioned by envy of the patrician sensibility, which birth has denied him. Lodovico has known and lost what Flamineo covets and apes; each is ruled by bitterness. In this opening scene Webster is initiating his plot but he is also teaching us how to read and differentiate character, how to interpret tones of speech. Infinitely more is conveyed in 62 lines than what is stated.

The Duchess of Malfi starts by exciting our discrimination differently: Webster sets up – a favourite device – two centres of action, challenging our response. Antonio tells Delio of the French court; the measured, formal pace of the verse captures exactly the sense of an ideal world:

> In seeking to reduce both State and people
> To a fix'd order, their judicious King
> Begins at home. Quits first his royal palace
> Of flatt'ring sycophants, of dissolute,
> And infamous persons, which he sweetly terms
> His Master's master-piece, the work of Heaven,
> Consid'ring duly, that a Prince's court
> Is like a common fountain, whence should flow
> Pure silver-drops in general.

[I i 5–13]

Bosola appears and his malcontent's nature is incisively
sketched by Antonio, the continuing measured quality of the
verse endowing the judgement with some authority. When the
Cardinal enters the medium changes to prose as Bosola
insistently dogs him, harrying for long-unpaid rewards for past
services; the Cardinal is cunningly evasive: 'You enforce your
merit too much' [*l.* 34]. The stark contrast is enforced by
Bosola's comparing the worlds of Cardinal and Duke not to a
self-perpetuating fountain but to 'plum trees, that grow crooked
over standing pools', their fruit sustaining 'crows, pies and
caterpillars'. With his departure, verse is resumed as Antonio
speculates whether Bosola's 'foul melancholy' will in time 'be
an inward rust unto the soul' [*l.* 78]. The pattern of prose
alternating with verse recurs in the next sequence as Ferdinand
exchanges witty banter with his circle of courtiers while
Antonio stands apart anatomising the Duke's 'most perverse
and turbulent nature', the serene tone of the opening recurring
only with his mention of the Duchess:

> Her days are practis'd in such noble virtue,
> That, sure her nights, nay more, her very sleeps,
> Are more in heaven, than other ladies' shrifts.
> > [I ii 126–8]

Having sounded his theme on the court, Webster presents us
with shifting perspectives contrasting our observations with his
characters' experiences to sharpen our judgement even as he
intimates the subjective limitations of perception. The dignity
and weight of the verse encourage a growing respect for
Antonio as a man of integrity and shrewd insight, careful
always (unlike Bosola) to be charitable; and yet we note that he
is invariably a man apart, his honesty and tone having no active
or creative engagement with the court; he will sustain till the
end the deference of the born servant. Bosola's caustic tone
springs from years of painful experience; Antonio's detachment
intimates a more protected existence (*in* the court but not *of* it)
which gives a credible motivation to his instant succumbing to
imagined disaster, once he is married and knows himself to be
the object of Ferdinand's hatred. And what of the Duchess?
Though to Antonio a model of princely virtue, she is soon

inviting him to a private assignation in the gallery, then being advised by her brothers to bear herself with seemly modesty and not play the libidinous widow. Nothing is for certain what it seems: we are sharply attentive to language but distrustful of all we hear. This meticulously prepares us for later Acts when, as we shall see, an art of verbal equivocation prevails, with punning and *double-entendres* of a high seriousness.

Generally the energy of Webster's verse is fitful, nervy, staccato, subservient always to the complex dramatic design of the play as a whole. The occasions when it expands into a lyrical outburst are so infrequent that they are dramatically distinctive. Consider Ferdinand's account of the tortures and protracted deaths he will inflict on the Duchess and her, as yet unknown, mate:

> I would have their bodies
> Burnt in a coal-pit, with the ventage stopp'd,
> That their curs'd smoke might not ascend to Heaven:
> Or dip the sheets they lie in, in pitch or sulphur,
> Wrap them in't, and then light them like a match:
> Or else to boil their bastard to a cullis,
> And give't his lecherous father, to renew
> The sin of his back.
>
> [II v 67–74]

What horrifies is the passionate attention to detail: these are no idle threats but the imaginings of a practised sadist who later in the play shows himself a connoisseur of lingering torments. Moments earlier he has urged the Cardinal to 'talk to me somewhat, quickly' to stop his mind imagining their sister 'in the shameful act of sin' and his fantasies of violence doubtless serve the same end; but relentlessly his mind returns to images of copulation and his sister's partner. The extravagant, obsessive sadism is the passion of a man who dare not admit to his true, incestuous desires. Our potential revulsion is circumscribed by our deepening psychological insight: Webster handles the episode with consummate tact.

A more usual source of sustained, indeed consciously-wrought, poetry occurs with the recounting of dreams or fables. Consider Act III of *The Duchess of Malfi* which ends with a scene framed by two such episodes. Cast forth from Ancona, the

Duchess suddenly recalls a recent dream of wearing her coronet of state when 'on a sudden all the diamonds / Were chang'd to pearls' [III v 14–15]: Antonio interprets the image emblematically as presaging tears, to which she responds enigmatically:

> The birds, that live i'th' field
> On the wild benefit of nature, live
> Happier than we; for they may choose their mates,
> And carol their sweet pleasures to the spring.
>
> [*ll.* 17–20]

Caught up on a wave of self-pity, the Duchess envisages a moment of pure natural joy free of the cares and petty pomp of statecraft. Through dream her mind has apprehended certain danger; she grasps at an image of bliss but Bosola's arrival immediately after compels her back to the world of stratagems and duplicity. Under arrest and separated from Antonio, she subsequently tells Bosola the fable of the salmon and the dogfish [*ll.* 124–40]. Prior to this she has grown hysterical when Bosola – quite unconsciously – transforms her vision of joy into an emblem of vulnerability and threat:

> I would have you tell me whether
> Is that note worse that frights the silly birds
> Out of the corn; or that which doth allure them
> To the nets?
>
> [*ll.* 98–101]

The fabling is an effort to instil calm, recover dignity, but with its intimations of the Last Judgement it shows her mind already dimly apprehending a new source of strength beyond her status as Duchess that will free her of self-pity and its attendant delusions.

A discussion of Webster's verse in all the examples explored is inseparable from a discussion of character and immediate context. In Webster's as in Shakespeare's tragedies the poetic artistry – the choice of style, image, rhythmic pulse – is at any moment the surest index of character; and yet one would apply that judgement differently to the two dramatists. Shakespeare's protagonists grow ever more deeply into understanding and acceptance of the complexities of self and the verse renders that process of change; most of Webster's protagonists are trapped in an emotional or intellectual vortex of which, till the last, they are but dimly conscious – 'mist' or 'maze' emblematises their innermost perception of self. The best they can be is true to the emotion of the moment, which is why they seem to live at their very nerve ends: feeling is their only gauge of existence.

3 THE HEROINES

The worlds of Webster's two tragedies are dominated by men and by patriarchal values: within his own dukedom the word of a Brachiano, Francisco or Ferdinand is law; the only superior authority is the Church and its sphere is seen to be more political than spiritual. The abiding concern is less with responsible rule than with power, aggrandisement, enhancing one's personal *will*. Both plays, as we have seen, carefully define this patrician consciousness as self-regarding, vicious because utterly shameless. Women have few opportunities in this world except as reflections of male rule: the virtuous because submissive wife, widow, mother or sister content to follow her lord's guidance and as such a valuable pawn in statecraft. To assert her independence is to be branded loose or shrewish. She must flatter her lord's *will* at the expense of her own. There is therefore great pathos in the Duchess's choice of a man of a different class and markedly different values for her second husband; but the freedom to be fully herself which she seeks in that marriage never extends beyond the privacy of their bedroom: her public self is still under her brothers' control. Vittoria is tempted away from an appalling arranged marriage by a man who seems sensitive to her feelings and womanhood and is quickly labelled 'whore' by the world at large and becomes an object of suspicion even to her lover. She finds herself the one means by which Brachiano's enemies can shake his patrician assurance; recovering his trust is a formidable challenge because he has been disturbed in the very roots of his being.

Whereas the men in Webster's plays are unconsciously trapped in their mental and spiritual condition, the heroines are self-evidently so by the social expectations of them as women. The alternative possibilities available to Vittoria are suggested through the other female characters: Isabella as devoted, all-suffering wife, inwardly raging against Brachiano's despotic treatment but struggling to accept it all as her duty; Cornelia, the inflexible moralist, who upholds the status quo and the primal value of the family to the eventual cost of her sanity; and Zanche who pursues sexual gratification with reckless abandon. Through trying to transcend these possibilities and find an acceptable identity, Vittoria is tragically doomed. It would be interesting to know whether Webster or his publisher chose to describe her on the title page as 'the famous Venetian Curtizan', for that is a judgement the play does not endorse. Similarly the portrayal of the Duchess is offset by Julia who eases the burden of matrimony to the tedious Castruchio by an ever-ready promiscuity, cheerfully describing herself as a great woman of pleasure [v ii 190]. If Vittoria and the Duchess earn our respect it is because they aspire to more than physical pleasure: they challenge the male prerogative to determine values in life.

That there could be another style to marriage is beautifully evoked by Webster simply through the tone of Act III Scene ii of *The Duchess of Malfi* where Antonio, Cariola and the Duchess desport themselves in the bedchamber. The quality of the teasing bespeaks a relaxed intimacy, trust and respect; the warmth of affection signifies a total emotional compatibility:

CARIOLA: Wherefore still, when you lie with my lady
           Do you rise so early?
ANTONIO: Labouring men
           Count the clock oft'nest Cariola,
           Are glad when their task's ended.
DUCHESS: I'll stop your mouth (*kisses him*).
ANTONIO: Nay, that's but one, Venus had two soft doves
           To draw her chariot: I must have another (*kisses her*).
                                                    [III ii 17–22]

It is an idyllic moment, the more poignant for the audience's sense of its fragility, knowing as they do that Ferdinand threatens to break into the room at any moment: the couple's serenity is permanently at hazard while the law lets his turbulence go unrestrained. The pathos in both tragedies illumines the social criticism.

Being conscious of the trap sprung about them poses the heroines an acute problem over expression. To speak out of that condition inevitably involves criticism of male authority, which risks being designated 'phlegmatic', 'shrewish', 'a witch', 'screech-owl', as if incapable of reasoned opinion. The great temptation is raillery – to pour forth a volley of abuse against the world and its cruel detractions; but that is to lose face and dignity since it lays one open to being dismissed as simply wearisome. It is the mark of the Duchess's absolute acceptance of her fate that in taking over control of organising her death from Bosola, she can foresee such an expectation of her and jestingly forestall it: 'I would fain put off my last woman's fault, / I'ld not be tedious to you' [IV ii 226–7].

Twice Vittoria is placed in a situation where railing would be an easy but fatal release of her feelings; both are instances where dramatic convention might lead an audience to expect fulsome tirades, since in each she is on trial arraigned as whore before Monticelso and Francisco [III ii], then Brachiano and her brother [IV ii]; and her judges unfairly stand as her accusers. The earlier episode is a terrifying display of the evils of the patrician privilege that we have been discussing. Monticelso asserts his office as Cardinal to dictate how the Court is to perceive Vittoria; he interprets her every phrase reductively to his advantage. Malice moves him, not objectivity. Vittoria trusts to her quick intelligence to rebuff him, clearly aware of the dangers of protesting at his methods. Courageously she refuses to let the trial be conducted in Latin showing she is not afraid for her reputation; questioning Monticelso's charity, 'Thou art seldom found in scarlet' [*l*. 71], she provokes him to a tirade on whores as 'worse than dead bodies' [*l*. 96], which she counters with studied innocence: 'This character 'scapes me' [*l*. 101]. Accused of effrontery for appearing without a 'mourning habit' at a trial for her husband's murder, she parries shrewdly:

Had I foreknown his death as you suggest,
I would have bespoke my mourning.
[*ll*. 122–3]

Monticelso dismisses that as 'cunning'; and Vittoria sees her
advantage and lays a trap for him: 'You shame your wit and
judgement / To call it so'. The Bible advises: 'Judge not lest ye
be judged' and she rightly opines that his deriding her 'just
defense' as 'impudence' is to leave himself open to criticism.
Humbly, with 'modesty and womanhood', she asks to be
treated with decorum, cruelly conscious that, to gain anything
approaching a sympathetic hearing, she must apologise for
what she has shown is her finest quality – her intelligence,
which has made her appear to 'personate masculine virtue'
[*ll*. 129–35]. Her very apology illustrates her quick-wittedness
to perceive the only way to prevent further unscrupulous
rejoinders.

Monticelso's anger at being bested in his own Court finds
expression in a ruthlessly straight question directed at catching
Vittoria off-guard in her moment of success by tricking her into
an admission of guilt or a lie: 'Who lodg'd beneath your roof
that fatal night / Your husband brake his neck?' [*ll*. 152–3].
Fortunately Brachiano answers and saves her. Baulked of his
prey, Monticelso savages Brachiano's reputation but the Duke
proves the prelate again wanting in charity and beneath
contempt. Once more Monticelso resorts to the raillery he tried
to force Vittoria to indulge in, but he cannot shake her inner
strength and sense of superiority: 'In faith my lord you might go
pistol flies, / The sport would be more noble' [*ll*. 210–11]. The
one recourse left him to silence her is to proceed to a sentence –
'confin'd / Unto a house of convertites' – and recommend
patience. Outrage at this unscrupulous turn of events finally
breaks Vittoria's self-command: she screams 'A rape, a rape!'
and curses her judges to the Cardinal's evident satisfaction, for
she has reduced herself at last to a type he can patronise: 'Fie,
she's mad – ... She's turn'd fury'. Vittoria perceives her
mistake and the danger of continuing to rail – 'O woman's poor
revenge / Which dwells but in the tongue!' [*ll*. 282–3]; with a
superhuman effort she denies herself the luxury of tears and
scorn, preferring the dignity of a controlled axiom that

contrives to transform her defeat into criticism of her judge's pettiness and vindication of her personal worth:

> Know this, and let it somewhat raise your spite,
> Through darkness diamonds spread their richest light.
> [*ll.* 292–3]

It is a magnificent performance, proof of an iron nerve and a dazzling brain – but superlative acting nonetheless (for we know she is guilty of adultery and of instigating the murders), aimed at achieving some measure of respect for herself as an individual; and she compels the court to take her seriously, as more than the sum of all the stereotypes with which they try to humiliate her. The decline of the trial into a savage travesty of justice is proof of her success: her judges have no precedent for coping with her. Yet that success makes her second trial in camera with Brachiano the more painful and demanding, for he now knows her to be an excellent actress and he seeks proof of her truth and fidelity. This time we know her innocence and sense the enormity of her position. Broken by imprisonment and by a want of trust where she most needs it, Vittoria lacks her former poise. Flamineo is no help with his intrusive prattle cynically questioning the value of everything. Her prodigious wit sees at once that the damning letter is a plot of Francisco's but she has to run the gamut of emotions in search of a tone that will convince Brachiano: calm reasoning, injured innocence, desperate renunciation, railing – she bewilderingly traverses them all in the space of a single tirade, before she collapses weeping on her bed vowing 'I'll not shed one tear more; – I'll burst first' [IV ii 128]. Sensing she has him in thrall, she risks a little girlish petulance:

> BRACHIANO: Are not those matchless eyes mine?
> VITTORIA: I had rather
> They were not matches.
> BRACHIANO: Is not this lip mine?
> VITTORIA: Yes: thus to bit it off, rather than give it thee.
> [*ll.* 133–5]

This is grotesque, a parody of feminine wiles. Yet precisely here at her least dignified moment in the play, she regains his

affection: 'Once to be jealous of thee is t'express / That I will
love thee everlastingly' [*ll*. 140–1]. The awareness of this
touches her to the quick:

> O thou fool
> Whose greatness hath by much o'ergrown thy wit!
> What dar'st thou do, that I not dare to suffer,
> Excepting to be still thy whore?
>
> [*ll*. 142–5]

His further cajoling deeply insults her: 'Am I not low enough?'
[*l*. 185]. It is a terrible moment of recognition when she sees
how little of her essential self is valued by her lover, how little of
what constitutes for us her brilliance and her individuality. Her
relationship with Brachiano continually frustrates her search
for a place where integrity might take root. She retreats into a
profound silence while the two men plot their future; in
dumbshow we watch her wedding procession: she speaks again
only when Brachiano lies poisoned – 'I am lost for ever'
[v iii 35]; his death deprives her of the one remaining value in
the relationship, his princely protection. As that apprehension
grows in her mind, she reaches a nadir of despair: 'O me! this
place is hell' [v iii 181]. All that is left her is the naked will to
survive.

Early in *The Duchess of Malfi* Ferdinand advises his sister to
abandon revels, 'A visor and a mask are whispering-rooms /
That were ne'er built for goodness' [i ii 256–7]. The
theatrical image is eerily prophetic of what is to be the
Duchess's innermost dilemma: how to balance the demands of
selfhood against those appertaining to her position. Once she is
married to Antonio, public life demands of each of them
consummate skill in acting because, instead of respecting a
balance of responsibilities, they choose to see the marriage as
the only reality and the world of the court as an illusion, play.
Just how dangerous this is is already presaged in their
courtship through a series of potent theatrical images: the
Duchess abdicates from certain responsibilities as though
divesting herself of roles she has outgrown or wearies of – her
title, her widowhood – that are to her now *vain* ceremonies. She
offers herself as simply woman for the marriage then, playfully,

assumes the emblematic stance of Blind Fortune. It is a touching gesture of virgin modesty as she encourages Antonio to lead her to bed but it also intimates the recklessness of their undertaking in hoping to break so easily with convention. The Duchess has pursued the courting under the guise of writing her will; to the idea of will as 'command' or 'appetite' is now added a third meaning, 'a last testament'. For all her charm and wit, she is playing with religion and in pursuing her infatuation for Antonio courting certain death. Always too on the periphery of her and our awareness lies thought of the stereotype that Ferdinand cast at her of 'lusty widow'. Given the complex political world of the play, that is too easy and too cruel a judgement but it is one against which it is difficult for her to define an integrity. Challenged in time by Ferdinand to explain herself, her only defence is that she has 'youth / And a little beauty' which fans his rage higher: he is the last person to whom she should address an appeal for imaginative sympathy. If she wins our pity, it is because we know how irksome to their souls it is that social necessity makes the Duchess and Antonio repeatedly enact 'a noble lie' [III ii 180] to protect the integrity of their union:

> O misery, methinks unjust actions
> Should wear these masks and curtains; and not we.
> [III ii 158–9]

Webster's source in Painter's *Palace of Pleasure* uncompromisingly condemns the heroine as wanton; the play is less prescriptive. Webster invents the character of Julia to define lustiness as his age understood it and creates a stagecraft that allows us both to value the marriage on its own terms and experience it in the larger political world of Church and State. Ironically from that omniscient standpoint it is the marriage that seems the illusion, the play, and the life of the court the painful, often hideous reality, a view that is the reverse of the lovers'. They are trapped by the willed uncertainty of their perceptions, never more so than when in the flurry of the moment the Duchess abandons her usual caution and tells the kindly-seeming Bosola the name of her secret husband. From that moment the private idyll is a lost Eden. It is a rash act but one like the courtship that Webster's art makes all-too-human. Emotionally fraught by Ferdinand's appearance and the rapid scheming for Antonio's departure in plausible circumstances for Ancona, the Duchess avidly welcomes Bosola's praise of her husband; lonely, she hungers for solace and she rewards his words of comfort with her trust. She has acted a part in the court for too long and too effectively to realise the consequences now of dropping her mask but they follow soon enough: she is rendered an outcast, arrested, imprisoned and left destitute of all her former roles to find a new identity. Alone of Webster's characters she will pass beyond the vortex of despair to find spiritual strength. In seeking to promote her right to be an individual and not a cypher, the Duchess like Vittoria is compelled inexorably to act, to feign in order to be true to what she sees as her quintessential self. At all points with admirable resourcefulness she resists the urge to rail even when she faces death. Vittoria opposed against her world a brilliant intellect; the Duchess a fearless resilience: unwisely but courageously she built an idyll of trust in a world of fierce duplicities; at the last she builds a Heaven within the bounds of Hell.

4 FLAMINEO AND BOSOLA

The malcontent is a curious phenomenon in Jacobean drama: a man of impoverished background but good education, hoping to advance himself into favour at court and therefore in part a sycophant, yet taking upon himself many of the qualities of the all-licensed fool to castigate the follies and iniquities of the society he moves in. As his hopes of preferment dwindle, his cynicism deepens. For a dramatist like Webster who wishes continually to shift an audience's perspective on to the action, the malcontent was an excellent device to challenge and shock; yet Flamineo and Bosola serve more than this function. They capture Webster's imagination because they seem to typify at its most extreme his view of human character as vacillating, arbitrary, at the mercy of circumstance and the individual will, and all despite a terrific energy of mind and penetrating insight. The roles require virtuoso performances both for the sheer range of tones their dialogue encompasses and even more for the complex psychology being defined; they are men who are at once inconsistent yet intensely self-aware, critical of others yet powerless to shape their own destinies to a desired end.

Flamineo's is a reductive mind because incapable of embracing any values other than material reward on any terms: 'Give me a fair room yet hung with arras, and some great cardinal to lug me by th' ears as his endeared minion' [v i 122–4]. He will make his sister's body 'a kind of path / To her and mine own preferment' [III i 37–8] and cuts short his brother's shocked tendentiousness, with the wry observation: 'Thou hast scarce maintenance / To keep thee in fresh chamois' [*ll.* 46–7]. His brain coins a ready answer to any check or challenge, undermining or misprizing other characters' protestations of honour, decency, integrity. Existence is to him nothing but the expression of appetite; against him we measure Vittoria's struggles to rise above the dictates of her will. He takes cruel advantage of her vulnerability and Brachiano's in the House of Convertites, instantly supposing her faithless and fostering the Duke's jealousy since, should it come to the lovers' parting, he needs must side with the stronger; then, when he realises that desperation at possibly losing her is rekindling Brachiano's infatuation, he plays the pander finely, coaxing, flattering, cocksure. Vittoria's final silence in the scene, which we sense as total revulsion, he sees as complacency and acquiescence:

So now the tide's turn'd the vessel's come about.
He's a sweet armful. O we curl'd-hair'd men
Are still most kind to women. This is well.
[IV ii 193–5]

Flamineo endlessly changes his style to reflect his lord's needs as he reads them, believing that '*Knaves do grow great by being great men's apes*' [*l.* 245]. His own words condemn him. Yet his quicksilver adaptability suggests his shrewdness, nerve, imaginative daring, vigorous wit – qualities he shares with his sister; his skill like hers is breathtaking; that he puts it to baser use enhances our perception of her growing intellectual scruple. His excitement at living, as he must, in the immediacy of the moment is in part its own reward but he can know bitter frustration and then that excitement pitches him into reckless bravado: pride in his capacity to adjust to the demands of the moment encourages him to take little thought of *consequences* when he publicly slaps Lodovico for playing fast and loose with his emotions [III iii], opens his soul to his supposed confederate Mulinassar, or stabs Marcello. Aping great men so much, he forgets momentarily he does not share their freedoms and privilege. His very nature makes him the architect of his own destruction. By the clever device of confronting him [v iv] with first the tableau of Cornelia preparing Marcello's corpse for burial and then the silent ghost of Brachiano, Webster intimates how conscience and fear of death haunt the periphery of his awareness; but they are apprehensions scarcely registered before being suppressed as his resilient self recovers control: 'This is beyond melancholy. I do dare my fate / To do its worst' [*ll.* 141–2]. The scene renders superbly the innermost workings of Flamineo's psyche.

When the King's Men acquired Marston's *The Malcontent* Webster wrote an Induction to the play. Marston shows a deposed duke, Altofront, assume the disguise of a 'court-gall' and the name Malevole as a way to bring about a revolution and recover his throne; restored, he discards his coarse-grained alter-ego. Playing a role serves his turn but no way affects his identity. Bosola similarly plays two parts in his person and struggles to reconcile them: his bitter railing is the measure of an impulse to good that cannot find active expression while he remains committed to a life at court which allows him to play only one role, 'intelligencer' (the very term intimates the cruel perversion of his strongest quality which success in that office requires). Antonio guides our understanding of Bosola; the first impression is that he is a second Flamineo:

> Indeed he rails at those things which he wants,
> Would be as lecherous, covetous, or proud,
> Bloody, or envious, as any man,
> If he had means to be so.

[I i 25–8]

But after Bosola imparts his view of the Aragonian brothers
which matches Antonio's own, the judgement is carefully and
more charitably framed:

> 'Tis great pity
> He should be thus neglected, I have heard
> He's very valiant. This foul melancholy
> Will poison his goodness . . . .
>
> [*ll*. 73–6]

The deep-rooted anguish of Bosola is defined further when
Ferdinand suborns him to play the spy by casually proffering
gold, that means so much to the one and so little to the other:

> I would have you curse yourself now, that your bounty,
> Which makes men truly noble, e'er should make
> Me a villain: O, that to avoid ingratitude
> For the good deed you have done me, I must do
> All the ill man can invent.
>
> [ı ii 195–9]

That he sees Ferdinand's magnanimity as an insult argues
Bosola's keen moral sense which he must suppress out of
financial need. Ferdinand, more cruelly than he can appreciate, advises him – 'Be yourself: / Keep your old garb of melancholy' (*ll*. 201–2) and be the abler spy. Ironically he has just
seduced Bosola from his better self, and now the Duke misprizes
the voice of conscience in him, urging his new spy to cultivate
his satirical vein as it will gain him 'access to private lodgings'
as courtly entertainment. Flamineo relishes playing the 'ape',
but it reduces Bosola to impotent rage and shame; where
Flamineo luxuriates in his mental agility, Bosola despises his.
When required as Ferdinand's agent to hound the Duchess to
despair, he cannot face her in his own person but assumes ever
more elaborate disguises. Conscience forbids he be himself.

And yet which is his true identity? The more conscience
goads him, the more promptly he submits to Ferdinand's
instruction; he seems possessed by voices that speak through
him with ventriloquial abandon. He praises Antonio to the
distraught Duchess as 'a most unvalu'd jewel / You have, in a
wanton humour, thrown away' [ııı ii 248–9]; but is this *at first*

the politic deception it subsequently becomes? When he learns
that Antonio is her secret husband, is his response studied
flattery or genuine astonishment, deceit to gain further
confidences or a kind of moral rapture?

> Do I not dream? Can this ambitious age
> Have so much goodness in't, as to prefer
> A man merely for worth . . .?
>   [*ll*. 276–8]

Antonio's fortunes stand revealed as the exact reverse of his
own, the fulfilment of all Bosola's aspirations. When next he
visits the Duchess, vizarded, to arrest her, their scene is a
chilling parody of this one. Again she seeks comfort but he
callously advises: 'Forget this base, low fellow' of 'barren,
beggarly virtue' [III v 116 and 121]. How much is this a
calculated meanness, the start of the torturing process? How
much is he activated by envy and desperation? Where does
acting end and feeling begin?

Our perplexity is fostered the better to appreciate what I
have called an art of equivocation which slowly suffuses the
dialogue from this point. It begins with Ferdinand's letter
requiring Antonio's 'head in a business' [III v 27], a threat the
Duchess quickly understands. This prepares us so that we
accurately interpret the dialogue uttered in darkness that leads
to the revelation of the dead hand. (Played thus we register less
the horror of the incident than the perverse mind that takes
such a connoisseur's pleasure in devising it.) We later
understand aright Bosola's wish that, when next he sees the
Duchess, 'The business shall be comfort' [IV i 134]. Yet how
are we to interpret Bosola's words after the discovery of the wax
effigies: 'Come, be of comfort, I will save your life' [*l*. 85] and
'Now, by my life, I pity you' [*l*. 87]? Is this a sadistic playing
with the Duchess's emotions or a crisis of conscience? There has
been considerable critical debate whether, when the Duchess
curses the heavens and Bosola responds 'Look you, the stars
shine still' [*l*. 99], he is cynically stressing human fallibility or
drawing her attention to the permanence of a divine order in
which she may trust fearlessly. But cannot the moment
embrace both possibilities? It is more profoundly tragic and in

keeping with the play's intricate network of ironies if Bosola throughout Act IV is seen *unconsciously* to set the Duchess on a path to grace along which he cannot follow. When next he goes to her his business is both death and comfort, since he intends to bring her, not as Ferdinand wishes to despair [IV i 115] but 'by degrees to mortification' [IV ii 176], to shock her into a state of torpor or numbed oblivion. Hence the madmen, the tombmaker, the bellman, the parade of coffin and cords. He thinks only of physical and mental release not of spiritual solace. But 'mortification' can also mean an ascetic disciplining of the body, an act of ritual cleansing, and this unexpectedly is the effect he produces. Far from rendering the Duchess insensible to pain, his process brings her 'well awake' [*l.* 224]. That he questions her – 'Doth not death fright you?' [*l.* 211] – shows his utter bewilderment that she can be vitally alert and *absolute* for death. He falls silent and leaves her to arrange the manner of her dying; it is he who is mortified, insensible. The stage action has one meaning for him and quite another for her and us, though he begins dimly to apprehend that other dimension of significance. The last sequence of the scene shows Bosola facing a bewildering conflict of moral choices. Ferdinand takes no satisfaction in the murder and refuses the promised reward, since to pay Bosola would be to admit his complicity in the deed; when Bosola presses him relentlessly he retreats from him and from the rising waves of his own conscience into madness: 'I'll go hunt the badger by owl-light: / 'Tis a deed of darkness' [*ll.* 332–3]. The Duchess, radiant in death, recovers consciousness sufficiently to utter 'Mercy' [*l.* 351]. The way of darkness and the way of light lie before him but, tragically, he cannot discriminate between them. He weeps in an anguish of indecision. Thinking of the recent murder, his mind senses a danger: 'That we cannot be suffer'd / To do good when we have a mind to it!' [*ll.* 357–8] but his introspection probes no further; he chooses resolute action and revenge, the way of the world, and dies in 'a mist' of errors. Conscience rots in Flamineo unused: he chooses to be the endless role-player 'varying of shapes' [IV ii 244] at the cost of all integrity. Conscience permeates Bosola's consciousness without to his chagrin finding there true habitation or a name. That he dies seeing himself as no more than 'an actor', a man

without fixed identity 'much 'gainst mine own good nature'
[v v 86], is his eternal shame.

5   WEBSTER'S PURPOSEFUL THEATRICALITY

The one vein of imagery that runs consistently throughout
Webster's tragedies developing and refining our perceptions of
the worlds and the characters he portrays relates to theatre,
performance, acting. It has been argued (initially by Lord
David Cecil) that Webster presents the world as a great stage of
actors because, pursuing a Calvinist philosophy, he saw life as
an illusion beside the Ultimate Realities of death, heaven and
hell. Certainly Webster, like many of his dramatist-
contemporaries, was conscious of the Morality tradition that
the Renaissance theatre inherited but to stress a Calvinist
approach risks losing a proper appreciation of the complexity of
sympathy and insight that has gone to the creating of Vittoria,
Bosola, Ferdinand; to ignore the carefully defined social and
political dimensions in the plays is to miss the pathos of
Flamineo's predicament, Isabella's or Julia's. Webster
meticulously avoids simple moral categories; and it is here that
the subtlety of his concern with the processes of theatre as
symbolic is most apparent. He repeatedly places his characters
in situations where they must act and the quality of their
response to this necessity sharpens our perception to a
remarkable degree of the innermost reaches of their psyches.
What impresses is the astonishing range of identities he so
defines and the intricacies of discrimination this excites in us.
When, for example, Isabella enacts a public separation from
Brachiano [II i 225–77], she speaks a script dictated already by
him [*ll*. 192–214]; as proof of her devotion, submissive to his
every whim, she plays the 'phlegmatic' duchess that she knows
it flatters his egoism to see her as being. She is always the
woman he chooses her to be, a model of duty, at the cost of those
'killing griefs which dare not speak' [*l*. 277]; and Brachiano
takes a cruel advantage of her. 'Acting' here with extreme

succinctness imparts a wealth of insights – social, psychological, emotional; paradoxically it shows us Isabella's *real* self.

Webster's purposeful theatricality extends further than this: he exploits the whole arsenal of styles and dramatic forms available to the Renaissance dramatist, but always to facilitate his psychological explorations, particularly into the nature of evil. Vittoria induces Brachiano to kill her husband and his duchess by recounting a studiedly allegorical dream; the murders are shown in dumb-show, an appropriate form since mime that, as here, has to convey a complicated narrative must proceed at a meticulously regulated pace, slower and more deliberate than action accompanied by dialogue and the resulting effect is otherworldly yet inexorable, timeless like nightmare. The dumbshows are conjured forth for Brachiano's exclusive viewing (which has the effect like the mime of distancing the horror); this allows us to study his mind as the deviser and director of these 'shows'. Murder to Brachiano is entertainment, an art whose refinements he savours richly: ''Twas quaintly done, but yet each circumstance / I taste not fully' [II ii 38–9]. This is the real horror of the scene – his gratuitous pleasure. The 'theatre' metaphor – the play and its aristocratic audience – renders with considerable economy the nature of Brachiano's sensibility and perverse imagination. Ironically his own death is to partake of nightmare: poisoned while jousting at his own wedding celebrations by a helmet that burns the flesh from his face in a 'show' of Francisco's creating. The idea of theatre brings a poetic logic to the developments of the plot, but invariably the prime focus is psychological: that the characters all converge on Brachiano's palace, that Flamineo is spurred on to release the bravado in his nature and Lodovico to uncage the beast in his, that the confederacy of the lovers, Flamineo and Zanche is riven apart by suspicion is wholly Francisco's doing. The last two acts represent the processes of mind that constitute his diabolical genius.

Similarly there is Ferdinand's method of attempting to harrow the Duchess's soul to despair in what is the most consciously wrought 'show' of all. As Inga-Stina Ewbank first argued, this partakes of the form, as a Jacobean audience would have been aware, of a court masque with its anarchic prologue

or anti-masque of madmen, its presenter (Bosola), its songs
and dance, presentation of a gift to an honoured member of the
audience whose character and destiny have been richly
celebrated in allegorical terms and in its final 'taking out' of
that honoured spectator from the audience to join in the revels.
Conventionally such a masque would have projected an emblematic vision of concord, harmony, peace; here the personi-
fications – tombmaker, bellman, executioners – represent
the faces of death. That all this is a grim parody of a wedding
masque implies Ferdinand offers it as a sardonic apology for his
failure to be present at the Duchess and Antonio's actual
ceremony; but it intimates yet more. As a metaphor for
Ferdinand's dark incestuous self it embodies his longing for a
perverse nuptial, an obsession he can stifle only with his sister's
death. By stylising the tortures into the ritual of the masque
Webster allows us to pass through the horror into an awareness
of the torment that is riving Ferdinand's soul and sanity apart.
Just as importantly the stylisation allows us to study the effect
of all the horror on the Duchess, for though Ferdinand can
order the place, time and method of her death, he cannot
control the mind and spirit in which she undergoes her
execution. He can shape her destiny only so far: in her mind she
is a free agent beyond the reach of his tyranny. Watching and
realising this disturbs Bosola profoundly, for it challenges every
level of his perception. Despite the powerful physicality of the
scene, the suspense, the crescendo of menace, it has been
scrupulously conceived and paced to fix our prime attention on
character. Again Webster's concern is with mind as process,
constantly in movement under the pressure of event. It is this
which transmutes his conscious theatricality into poetry *of* the
theatre: the stage action is total metaphor.

6 DEATH

Webster was the contemporary of the metaphysical poets and,
while it would seem an exaggeration to describe his outlook as

Calvinist, his art is undeniably metaphysical in style and content. His purposeful theatricality creates for drama witty conceits of the highest order and his ultimate purpose is to show how individuals shape their souls for the hereafter. That is the essence of his tragic vision; his haunting ability to delineate the effects of dying on consciousness is compassionate not morbid, because he possesses an extraordinary skill to bring our whole knowledge of a character sharply into our awareness as his or her consciousness ceases to function for ever. The great Aragonian Cardinal makes a mockery of his calling; his true self behind the crimson splendour is secretive, insidious, 'rotten and rotting others' [IV ii 318]; disgraced in the circumstances and manner of his death, he chooses to be 'laid by, and never thought of' [v v 90]. Ferdinand, stabbed by his intelligencer who has held the mirror up to his nature showing that his heart is a hollow grave [IV ii 317], dies recognising that his schemes have led inexorably to this end, that what he deemed his own brilliance has undermined his sanity, his will, his life: 'Like diamonds we are cut with our own dust' [v v 73]. As his mind centres on an image that expresses his perception of his life's achievement, it sits in judgement on itself and presages its inevitable future. This is but a moment's apprehension but Ferdinand has looked into his soul and knows it to be a dead thing.

Both tragedies stress the high seriousness of the final deaths by placing them in contexts that once again are overtly theatrical. The Cardinal, wishing to dispose privately of Julia's body, has bid his retainers on oath to refrain from coming to him on any pretext and adds:

> It may be to make trial of your promise
> When he's asleep [i.e. Ferdinand], myself will rise, and feign
> Some of his mad tricks, and cry out for help,
> And feign myself in danger.
>
> [v iv 13–16]

When he does so cry out in an ecstasy of genuine pain, the courtiers appear '*above*' and joke about the excellence of his acting. The effect of this in performance is to deflect our attention away from the death-throes simulated by the

performers playing the Cardinal, Ferdinand and Bosola
(potentially grotesque) to concentrate on the language through
which Webster conveys the characters' agony of soul. The end
of *The White Devil* is yet more daring where Flamineo himself
mimics a conventional theatrical death as yet another trial of
Vittoria's trustworthiness. He proposes a suicide pact;
cheerfully agrees to be the first to be shot; frames a death-
speech full of contempt for the world and the grave; welcomes a
violent end 'For from ourselves it steals ourselves so fast / The
pain once apprehended is quite past' [v vi 115–16]; 'killed', he
luxuriates in bizarre rhetoric that closely parodies Webster's
own metaphysical style:

> My liver's parboil'd like Scotch holy-bread;
> There's a plumber, laying pipes in my guts, it scalds.
>
> [v vi 141–2]

When Vittoria refuses to follow suit, he leaps to his feet
revealing it was all a nasty trick. (Had she killed herself, he
would presumably have claimed the treasure Brachiano has
bequeathed her; his last thoughts previously were of her
new-won 'bounty'.) Within moments brother and sister are
trussed up as Lodovico and Gasparo put them to a hideous,
protracted death in earnest. Webster has set himself a formidable
challenge to find an apt and convincing tone to distinguish
bravery from bravado. Lodovico taunts them in the hope that
they will rail and demean themselves, but Flamineo is not to be
provoked: 'Wouldst have me die, as I was born, in whining?'
[*l.* 193] and Vittoria is equally adamant: 'I will not in my death
shed one base tear, / Or if I look pale, for want of blood, not
fear' [*ll.* 223–4]. As their enemies strike, they assume a wry
indifference:

> VITTORIA: 'Twas a manly blow
>   The next thou giv'st, murder some sucking infant,
>   And then thou wilt be famous.
> FLAMINEO: O what blade is't?
>   A toledo, or an English fox?
>
> [*ll.* 230–3]

Her tone awakens him for the first time in the play into respect: 'Th'art a noble sister, / I love thee now' [*ll*. 239–40]; but pain has carried her consciousness beyond thought of him or her tormentors. She suddenly knows herself in a fleeting moral vision as her ebbing vitality makes it impossible to strive for a remedy: 'My soul, like to a ship in a black storm, / Is driven I know not whither' [*ll*. 246–7]. Flamineo tries various tones in which to die, the cheering, the moral, the satirical, before the urgency of the moment ('I recover like a spent taper, for a flash / And instantly go out') impels him to find his truth to experience within: 'at myself I will begin and end' [*l*. 256]. He, the consummate actor, proudly accepts death and its consequences in terms of that, acting, his only continuing reality: 'I have caught / An everlasting cold. I have lost my voice / Most irrecoverably' [*ll*. 268–70]. Dying, he is the loquacious comedian rudely silenced. His wit, resilient to the bitter last, wins our respect. Brilliantly Webster frames his poetic art to define with extraordinary precision each mind's perception that the sum of its achievements is *nothing*. Unused, the moral imagination stirs in the characters only to confront them with images of a void and of non-being. That it stirs at all is what invests them with tragic dignity. Having lived to the limit of their senses in and for the moment, they have a rare perception of the moment in its final passing.

The deaths so far considered are all precipitate, fearful for the haste that urges the dying consciousness to a last reckoning. The Duchess has time to find a proper decorum. Surrounded by madmen, she is still, composed; confronted by a satirical tombmaker she can quietly jest, like Cleopatra with the clown that brings her the asps, showing her complete mastery of herself; the display of the coffin and the singing of a dirge that render Cariola hysterical leave her concerned only for her servant's welfare (the command to attend to her children's health and prayers has its pathos but is also a charitable gesture to focus Cariola's distracted mind on a specific task). Alone with her murderers, she enquires after the mode of her death, forgives them, instructs herself to be brief, arranges the disposal of her corpse and chooses in humble piety to die kneeling, since 'heaven gates are not so highly arch'd / As princes' palaces' [IV ii 232–3]. She has divested herself of everything that constitutes her human identity – her titles of duchess, wife, mother, mistress (and as she recognises in this last act even that of sister); and she clings to no final image that might define herself in the face of the potential void. Her abnegations are absolute yet her consequent repose, physical and emotional, betokens a grandeur of soul. It is a perfectly judged theatrical effect to make sheer stillness, the refusal to act even in the face of unrelieved horror, a metaphor for transcendence. Webster refuses to sentimentalise his achievement, any more than Shakespeare does with his reconciliation of Lear and Cordelia: the Duchess's spirit advises Bosola to learn mercy and Antonio to be mindful of his safety and fly his fate [v iii]; both are to cease trying to resolve the quarrel with her brothers. Neither man can achieve the abnegation of self that this would require. At the moment of his death Antonio comes to share her perception and bids his son 'fly the courts of princes' [v iv 71]. But Bosola quite loses touch with her example: dying, his thoughts are only of the 'deep pit of darkness' in which, 'womanish and fearful, mankind live' [*ll*. 101–2]. The Duchess inhabited a veritable, not metaphorical, 'pit of darkness' and, being fearless, rose above such a disparaging estimate as 'womanish'. But she went a metaphysical progress none dared follow, trusting to find the necessary strength within: for the audience that is the tragedy and the challenge.

PART TWO: PERFORMANCE

7 INTRODUCTION: FINDING AN APPROPRIATE STYLE FOR WEBSTER

Webster poses the modern theatre-director formidable problems. There is much that a contemporary Jacobean audience could be assumed to know which a twentieth-century audience needs explained; Webster did not need to waste valuable stage-time on such explanations but a director today must find a way of enlightening his audiences without significantly disrupting the rhythm of the play as Webster conceived it. Many of these problems centre on social attitudes that are now alien to us: the *absolute* authority of a man of ducal status, his patrician sensibility recognising only the papacy as superior in command; the intricate gradations of a class-system rigidly adhered to, that made Brachiano's pursuit of Vittoria or the Duchess's wooing of Antonio an immediately shocking and dangerous challenge to the status quo for a Jacobean spectator, for all that in the second case Antonio is exceptionally well-educated, utterly honest and, as the opening scene shows, adept in the arts of chivalry and courtesy (both aristocratic virtues); then there is the question of a woman's social position, whatever her status, as always subject to her father, husband or brother and quite without authority except when widowed and protecting the interests of a young heir till his coming of age (both situations allowed women of high birth to be used as pawns in dynastic scheming by their male relatives). Webster has often been accused of being careless in his plotting, especially in his expositions, yet these social attitudes and values which are the mainspring of the tragic action in both plays were so much a part of the fabric of Jacobean thinking that they did not require detailed definition. Today some means must be found to convey their force.

Further the plays take on trust without seeing the need to

explain the baroque sensibility of the age, what Emrys Jones
has brilliantly described as 'the rampant rationalism and the
organized insanity . . . and along with them the sheer
unnerving creepiness (as it may appear to a disaffected eye) of
baroque Catholicism'. Ferdinand, Brachiano, Francisco and
Lodovico pursue a logic of the individual will that abuses
human feeling and ultimately human life; learning does not win
Antonio respect from anyone his social superior except the
radically minded Duchess, while learning in Bosola
degenerates into crabbed satire or a perverse bookishness. The
characters, almost without exception, long for sensual abandon
as proof that they are genuinely living, several like Julia and
Zanche pursuing it with a frantic desperation, out of a fear of
death; with the exception of the Duchess's private life with
Antonio, apprehension is the tenor of mind in which the
characters habitually live till the moment death actually
confronts them, which is what gives the verse and the dramatic
action their peculiar nervous energy. It would be wrong for a
director to view this as melodramatic sensationalism: the tone
is much more complex in its social, cultural and spiritual
implications. A director and cast have to be mindful of the
psychological rather than physical action which shapes the
meaning of particular scenes. Webster delights in spectacle and
sensational events less for their intrinsic emotional value than
for the way they allow him incisively to define the characters'
innermost psychological and spiritual condition. The
passionate physicality of the plays is repeatedly a metaphor
with deep metaphysical resonances. The worldly and the
other-worldly are strangely integrated in Webster's vision and a
director must respect that fusion as fundamental to an
understanding of Webster's theatrical artistry and dramatic
method.

Given these difficulties, it is not surprising that the history of
the tragedies in performance is not a wholly satisfying one. The
problem is essentially one of style and discipline: a director has
to find a way of realising on stage a specific 'period' sensibility
but not to an extent where the detail becomes fussy and
intrusive, getting in the way of an audience's imaginative
engagement with the plays' metaphorical dimensions. In an
age of cinema and television, where generally the visual has

primacy over the spoken, it is difficult for a director to realign his priorities; yet to allow the visual to dominate a production can make the plays seem merely studies in decadence and reduce Webster's dramatic method seemingly to a crude lurching from one sensational climax to the next with little thought of narrative progression or consistency of character-portrayal. If audiences are physically nauseated by the realism of Lodovico making Italian cutworks in Flamineo and Vittoria's guts (Robert Helpmann's costume as Flamineo in a 1947 production of *The White Devil* concealed a bag of sheep's intestines that seeped out during his final speeches), then they will lose concentration and miss imaginatively engaging with Vittoria's contemplation of eternity which the ecstasy of pain brings her to, Flamineo's sudden revaluation of his relationship with his sister at the moment of her extinction and, in marked contrast, the evil of Lodovico dying exultant in having achieved his masterpiece in organising this carnage. The danger with the overly visual approach in production is that it encourages the actors to seize on the sheer nervous intensity of the verse and overact in order to make an impact. This inevitably sets at risk the psychological intricacies of scenes that require consummately sensitive ensemble playing. A proper style for Webster in performance must willingly embrace the discipline of the stylised in terms of both design and acting technique.

A good way of introducing the four productions chosen for detailed study would therefore appear to be through the style of design each adopted. Frank Dunlop staging *The White Devil* for the National Theatre in 1969 invited Piero Gherardi to be his designer. Gherardi had previously worked with Fellini on several of his films; his preferred manner was ornate, decadent, surreal. His permanent set suggested a series of monumental, crumbling walls of stone, yet the layout imitated the levels, entrances, discovery and playing spaces of the Elizabethan theatre which allowed a rapid progress of the action. It conveyed no immediate metaphorical connotations except perhaps through the ancient rocks the suggestion that these Renaissance aristocrats were at one in spirit with the world of the more vicious emperors of Roman antiquity, and that Rome, the so-called holy city, was in truth a place of sinister crimes and covert vice. If the setting made no immediately powerful impact, the costumes did: they followed the line of Renaissance attire for men and women but were made in unusual, modern fabrics – exotic lace and minutely-pleated tulle, that made the actors seem like giant butterflies or moths. The dominant image was of creatures mesmerised and all-too-quickly consumed by their own lusts like the proverbial moth drawn to its extinction by the candleflame. This complemented well Webster's theme of the ephemerality of power, pomp and pleasure; and it was shocking to discover that such gorgeousness without masked viciousness within and spiritual vacuity.

Where the design-concept failed was, interestingly, with Vittoria. Her hair was teased out and curled into a cobra-like hood that gave her head the look of the Medusa aureoled with writhing snakes. The problem was that this instantly judged the character as a she-devil, a threatening basilisk, and it compelled Geraldine McEwan to play Vittoria as the complete whore, mistress of coquetry, wantonly luring Brachiano to his destruction. This was to simplify Webster's complex moral stance throughout the opening acts: the strong, critical statement made by the designer prevented the audience engaging imaginatively with Vittoria's dilemma and moral confusion. She is at first eager for Brachiano's sexual advances but fearful of the consequences; she boldly intimates to her lover how murder might make their relationship easier socially but is stung to the quick by her mother's tirade against adultery; her husband is gross, her lover attractive, yet her brother's pandering chatter intimates that all relationships are a matter of political strategy or sexual gratification. Vittoria's consciousness is harassed with moral choices and a ready judgement of her is impossible. Gherardi also staged a moment of spectacle in the trial scene that again undermined the complexity of Webster's art: Vittoria appeared in a severe gown and cowl of brilliant white; when her indignation flared up at Monticelso's abuse of his position as judge, the dress on the sudden turned inside out leaving her clad now in an equally vibrant red. Astonishment at the ingenuity of the effect quite disturbed one's concentration on the psychological intricacies of the trial; more importantly the image of the 'scarlet woman' invited us to see Vittoria as her judges see her at the precise moment that Webster asks us to look beyond her guilt and see in her a kind of integrity and sense of fair justice battling to win recognition. Throughout the designer compounded the chauvinist attitude to Vittoria shared by the male characters in the play rather than seeking to complement Webster's more compassionate (because morally more sensitive) assessment.

Michael Lindsay-Hogg's production of *The White Devil* (Old Vic, July 1976) used a text prepared by Edward Bond that moved the action forward in time into the present day. The setting by John Gunter was simple, stylish, in a uniform brown with touches of Art Deco: we were in the lobby of an expensive hotel with the characters making their entrances through revolving doors on either side of the proscenium. The costumes were quiet, beautifully cut, suggestive of a wealth that was so innate a part of life that the characters felt no need to make an effect. Brachiano, Isabella, Francisco, Monticelso were aristocrats to the core, luminaries of the 'jet set'; Vittoria (Glenda Jackson) and Flamineo intelligent 'outsiders'. Many critics disliked the studied coolness of the production, considering it lacked the seething decadence of Webster's imagining. Yet that decadence manifests itself largely through the inner chaos of the characters and it was profoundly disturbing when the chic persons of this production got caught up in vicious desires or were seized by an animal lust for violence. Isabella's shock at her husband's ill-treatment and her total submissiveness were convincing for their isolation in a world that, for all its seeming urbanity, leapt with avidity at any chance to pursue revenge; these beautiful beings with their doll-like faces set in repose were hungry for opportunities to express their true selves in cruelty. As a consequence of this the production succeeded well where it might have been expected to fail. James Villiers, an unctuously suave Brachiano, became a genuinely frightening ghost, his face and scalp half-eaten away by poison, through the stark contrast of a modern gentleman transformed into a timeless symbol of mortality. There was nothing comic about this apparition and Flamineo's subsequent dismissal of its warning presence was felt to be the reckless, if daring gesture Webster intimates. Similarly when the cycle of retributive murders began, it seemed wholly apt that these exquisites should avoid modern weapons inflicting instantaneous death in preference for the swords and daggers of olden times, that, wounding, leave the victim lingering in agony. The production and its related design-concept were meticulously thought through: this was a modern realisation that took care to stay faithful to the spirit of the original in its quest for a viable style.

Peter Gill directing *The Duchess of Malfi* (Royal Court Theatre, January 1971) carried austerity to an extreme, aided by William Dudley (setting) and Deirdre Clancy (costumes). The company were first seen sitting on two rows of plain deal chairs; behind them the brick wall of the stage had been left exposed, while to either side was a row of peeling, dilapidated, matchwood doors. The characters were dressed uniformly in acid yellow, the costumes intimating the simplest lines of Jacobean dress. Gill seemed to be stressing the characters' common humanity and a common mortality; and the programme quoted what the setting realised: 'I know death hath ten thousand several doors / For men to take their exits' [IV ii 219–20]. Death here was the Great Leveller. Actors not appearing in a scene were used like a chorus in groupings to indicate a sense of place; they also vocalised the sound and musical effects throughout. The matter of rank was not ignored despite the costumes: the Duchess and her brothers in the opening scenes were carried in by the chorus of actors, held aloft like venerated processional images. The production had a fast-moving choreographic sweep that gave the narrative line of the play great clarity. Some critics found it all cold, unimpassioned, because, clearly, they found the style alien to their expectations of how Renaissance drama should be staged; Gill borrowed considerably from the techniques of recent experimental fringe theatre, which in 1971 were comparatively new and startling innovations, especially when applied like this to the classical repertoire. But such techniques were finely disciplined to make the audience's imaginative response to what they saw and heard part of the whole creative process: we engaged immediately with the psychological and metaphysical dimensions of Webster's play. Because there was no literal rendering on-stage of the trappings of Renaissance wealth and power, we could focus more precisely on how the characters' use of jewels, foodstuffs, rich clothing, make-up as images in their speeches defines their personal spiritual values and condition. The visual austerity on-stage excited a profound attention to Webster's language so that much of one's experience of the play was perceived by what the poet Yeats called 'the eye of the mind'. The stylisation allowed the verse a rich dramatic life.

Philip Prowse, a designer–director, is renowned for his creative use of spectacle: he has a considerable gift for bringing a historical era to life in powerful visual terms. The opening sequence of his production of *The Duchess of Malfi* for the National Theatre (Lyttleton, July 1985) was a virtuoso display of his personal style. We were in the long hall of a vast, baroque palace, whose white walls were overhung with a vaulted ceiling that reached up to some unimaginable height whence a cold light spilled down on a procession of all the noble characters to church; the tolling of a single great bell intimated along with the sumptuous black costumes that they were attending the obsequies of the Duchess's late husband. It was a weird slow march moving in time with the bell but punctuated with moments of stillness in which the cries of peacocks could be heard. Tense, stiff-backed and with glazed eyes the Aragonian family moved inexorably onward, compelling Bosola, anxious for an interview with the Cardinal, to keep scuttling out of their path. Antonio, bowing repeatedly, supervised their progress with the eye of one skilled in devising state ceremonies. Here at once were images of power, rank, wealth; yet in that undeviating advance across the stage, there were intimations too of the self-willed relentlessness that impels the characters steadily towards their demise: the court rituals in the play are all part of a great dance of death. There was the further implication that piety was for most of these characters an empty, formal ritual. For later scenes the wall slid back to reveal a series of chambers decorated with glass cases full of silver crucifixes, chalices and reliquaries, while above were Bernini-like statues of saints caught in the raptures of martyrdom or of spiritual enlightenment – images of piety, ecstasy and death, but frozen in marble or imprisoned in glass, not vital, meaningful emblems for the individuals who passed their lives in such surroundings. To see the Cardinal groping amorously with Julia in that setting was shocking; the more so

in that Prowse kept a silent, observing figure on stage
throughout the action, clad in a black cowl and habit, whom
one gradually realised was Death patiently waiting his moment
to strike. He was the omniscient witness of human folly, the
yardstick against which to measure every action. Despite his
flair for spectacle, Prowse cut the dumbshow of the Cardinal's
investiture and the Duchess's banishment at Ancona; instead
the Duchess was confronted by an angry Cardinal who slapped
her in the face and on the instant the walls of the set reversed, as
if moving on 'strange geometrical hinges' [iv ii 221), statues
and display cases vanished and the Duchess, stripped of all the
panoply of state, confronted the bleak white walls of her prison
where Death was to become her comforter and companion. The
visual imagery of the production was undeniably powerful but
to an extent that often rendered Webster's verbal imagery
redundant: oddly enough, nothing quite lived up to one's expectations after the brilliant opening, since Prowse did not use
Webster's text to develop the implications that he had made
one sense there. Also the production had the effect of en-
couraging a kind of imaginative lassitude in the audience: the
visual effects *explained* so much about the characters' moral
complexion and the values of the world they inhabited that the
play ceased to involve the audience in a process of discovery
through their creative response to the way Webster shapes
language in relation to action. The presence of Death was an
irony that lost its force by becoming too familiar, his figure
failing in time to bring an air of menace and danger to the
action. The idea might have worked had the role been played
by a mime or a dancer whose movements would have been of a
different order of theatricality; as it was, the actor was too *solid*,
too much a part of the social rather than the metaphysical
world to be a serious threat except perhaps in the last act. The
production-style, though good at evoking a feeling of historical
time and place, ultimately proved rather cramping, largely
because Prowse seemed reluctant to respect his audiences'
intellectual and imaginative power to interpret for themselves
and sense subtleties of nuance and implication in language. This
was in consequence a lavishly conceived but somewhat flawed
production.

A.   The Wedding Procession (V.i) from Frank Dunlop's production of *The White Devil* showing Piero Gherardi's designs.   Photograph © Zoë Dominic.

B.   The trial scene (III.ii) with Geraldine McEwan as Vittoria and John Moffat as Monticelso.   Photograph © Zoë Dominic.

C. The trial scene (III.ii) in Lindsay-Hogg's production of *The White Devil* with Patrick Magee as Monticelso and Glenda Jackson as Vittoria. Photograph © John Haynes.

D. The suicide pact (V.ix) with Glenda Jackson and Jack Shepherd as Flamineo. Photograph © John Haynes.

E. Peter Gill's production of *The Duchess of Malfi:* the Duchess (Judy Parfitt) with the madmen.   Photograph © John Haynes.

F. The Duchess's death.   Photograph © John Haynes.

G. Philip Prowse's staging of *The Duchess of Malfi* showing the setting for the
Duchess's court with from left to right: Eleanor Bron as the Duchess, Greg
Hicks as Antonio and Selina Cadell as Cariola. Photograph © John Vere
Brown.

H. The setting for act IV with shadow effects and the ominous presence of Death,
the cowled figure on the left. Ian McKellen (centre) as Bosola prepares to
show the Duchess the 'dead' body of Antonio. Photograph © John Vere
Brown.

8   FRANK DUNLOP'S PRODUCTION OF *THE WHITE DEVIL*, 1969

Geraldine McEwan's Vittoria Corombona in Frank Dunlop's production was in every detail of her performance 'the famous Venetian Curtizan'. Her walk was eloquently seductive; her eyes were constantly heavy-lidded with satiety and appetite; she was pretty and vicious; her voice could swoop in languorous drawl or lash out with icy venom. Hers was the infinite variety of the born coquette: tantalising, predatory, blowing warm or cold as it suited her turn. It was a consistently sustained reading but one that, as already stated, inevitably missed much of the character-potential of the role, especially in the early acts. This was compounded by the director's unwillingness to see the heroine as in any way the victim of social circumstance and the masculine values of the world she lives in. This Vittoria had already chosen her role in life at the outset of the play; if she went along with Flamineo's game to entrap Brachiano, it was as a convenient step to further her own ambitions. To make sense of Flamineo's lines where he cajoles Vittoria into Brachiano's arms, McEwan *played* the tender, frightened innocent, the better to excite the Duke's lust. She was always the actress, indeed that was part of her mesmeric fascination. A consequence of this was that the trial scene lacked the tension that evolves from the audience's uncertainty over when Vittoria is acting and when speaking in earnest. It was not a woman of considerable intelligence that Vittoria became for us here, seeing and pressing her advantage over her judges, but one made clever by shameless bravado; we saw the effrontery of an actress in full control of her technique. But there is more to Webster's Vittoria in this scene than sheer nerve; danger is sharpening her perception of herself and of her own intrinsic worth.

If McEwan's reading seemed wayward at first, it did grow in stature as the play advanced, because the portrayal allowed her to find deeper and deeper levels of pathos in Vittoria's predicament. In the House of Convertites she presented the heroine as utterly at a loss as to what role to play, what tone to adopt to revive Brachiano's affection. The consummate actress played over again the gamut of her emotional ploys to no avail and fell silent in sheer desperation at discovering the limits of her power in the face of Brachiano's consuming jealousy. It was not the total existential despair that can be read into this moment in the action but McEwan did suggest a woman starting on the thorny path to self-awareness; and her performance continued to build on the implications of this. The dying Brachiano's refusal to kiss her lest she be afflicted proved belatedly to her the seriousness of his affection, causing her in turn to reassess her feelings for him and discover love in the instant of its loss. Her frantic attempt to break through the circle of murderers in response to his calling out her name in his death throes was most moving. Similarly after all the hysteria of the mock suicide with Flamineo, brother and sister grew into a more tender relation together, as if the imminence of death brought a clarity of perception, purging away selfish intent and pettiness. Though Geraldine McEwan opted initially for a showy exhibitionist interpretation of Vittoria that rather simplified Webster's conception of the role, she did invest her with tragic dignity at the last by showing her learn through suffering and lose the value of emotional scruple. Chained to a rock by Lodovico, she expired with a death-rattle that galvanised her entire body as if her soul recoiled from its vision of sailing into a black void and she clung rapaciously to life. This was a consistent reading of Vittoria as complete sensualist that achieved in intensity what it lacked in subtlety.

Perhaps this was a sensible decision on Miss McEwan's part: she undeniably created a memorable impression where most of the other performers seemed dwarfed by the costumes and production-effects. Derek Godfrey as Brachiano gave a lightweight performance, missing the nastiness of the man, his quickness to scent an injury to himself, his fury, and his hell-bent recklessness; but then in most of his crucial scenes Godfrey was robbed of the central focus by scenic displays. The first, astonishing vision of Vittoria in her extravagant costume and towering wig prevented him establishing the Duke's infatuation as fatal in its abandonment to excess; in the murders of Isabella and Camillo it was the two dumbshows that were held centre stage and Brachiano was treated as merely a device to facilitate their exposition. It seemed the director's way with the character of Brachiano to treat him as simply functional – the man whose lust sets the action going. Webster, however, is fascinated by the type of patrician mind that is a law unto itself and he takes care to depict it in some depth for its passionate ruthlessness; and he creates a deliberate structural balance in the play by contrasting Brachiano with Lodovico and Francisco, the former under the sway of a passionate nature that verges on the manic, the other given over to a ruthlessness that is cunningly masked by guile and diplomacy. Because the director was fundamentally preoccupied with incident rather than with character, this instructive pattern of contrasts did not make itself felt. Brachiano's only notable scenes were those involving his death, which allowed for spectacular treatment: the tournament was staged as a display of aggressive *machismo* fencing, the several consecutively staged bouts being choreographed in time with amplified bull-like snorts from the contenders which were suddenly disrupted by a shrill, falsetto cry when the Duke realised his visor was poisoned. Later, separated from Vittoria and realising the monks officiating at his bedside were his enemies in disguise, he became delirious with panic which his lips now scarcely had strength to express; on Gasparo's command that Brachiano be strangled in private, Lodovico took a grim pleasure in doing so with the aid of the rosary and crucifix that he had but lately used while pretending to administer Holy Unction to the Duke.

It was a pity that the pattern of contrasts was not adequately realised, as Francisco was given a particularly sensitive reading by Anthony Nicholls. An older actor of considerable presence, he took care amidst the flamboyant movement of the production to be still, immensely self-contained. In his plotting revenge when in IV i and IV iii he manoeuvred his enemies and his pawns into position, only his eyes and the deepening tones of his voice intimated his growing satisfaction especially with his own performance in changing shapes so skilfully as to trick Monticelso and Lodovico into furthering his cause. His disguise as Mulinassar he took on with great relish; to regular patrons of the Old Vic at this time there were unmistakable echoes of Olivier playing Othello. The element of parody worked well in developing the theme of conscious role-playing as a calculated political strategy which recurs throughout the last act, while the wit inherent in the performance here was an incisive way of conveying Francisco's absolute assurance of his power to succeed. It was a finely judged portrayal, sensitive to Webster's demands for the role, that might have been imitated to advantage by some of the other actors, especially Edward Woodward as Flamineo.

Flamineo as the role-player *par excellence*, changing his manner and tone with dazzling virtuosity to suit every occasion, is the closest in conception amongst Webster's characters to those popular creations of Marston like Antonio and Malevole, who are commentators on, organisers of and participators in the action, forever standing back to judge their performances the better to adapt to changing circumstance. Flamineo has a chameleon-like mind which he deploys with a barbed wit; properly played with the actor relishing the opportunities of the part as much as the character relishes his own skill and technique as an actor, he is a source of considerable intellectual energy and humour. Unfortunately the production valued physical action more highly than mental, and Woodward was not given adequate stage-time to be expansive; his speeches were delivered at such breakneck speed as to be at times almost unintelligible. Certainly Flamineo lives at his nerve ends and occasionally and disastrously overreaches himself through emotional excess with Lodovico [III iii] and with Mulinassar (throughout Act V), but he is more than the frenetic, anxiety-racked individual Woodward created. Flamineo is ambitious, determined to the extent that he grows desperate at times when he senses he is being baulked of his objective as in the House of Convertites, but he is also the mordant observer of court ways; it is because he despises so much aristocratic pretension that he aspires to rank and position, judging himself to be intellectually more worthy and astute than so many born nobles. Ironically, of course, circumstance proves him no real match for Brachiano and certainly no equal of Francisco. Woodward's Flamineo reached after the full potential of the role only in the final scene where the element of spectacle involved allowed him to give a more complex reading: 'I am not wounded: / The pistols held no bullets: 'Twas a plot' [v vi 147–8] was a whoop of sardonic triumph both comic and menacing after his quite convincing death-agonies and here he was at one with the Flamineo who, as actor, is both mesmeric and dangerous. Equally effective, after the ensuing bitter denunciation of Vittoria as treacherous woman incarnate, was his recognition of Vittoria's true worth as she faced death with nothing but scorn for her murderers. Brother and sister both at the last achieved the aristocratic temper they had erstwhile aspired to.

By seeing *The White Devil* as a vehicle for an exhibition of high camp, Frank Dunlop robbed a potentially fine cast of the chance to explore Webster's psychological artistry. His accent fell relentlessly on the play as a narrative about the intricacies of decadence and the characters were simplified to facilitate the projection of that view. But Webster, while fascinated and appalled by the *products* of decadence – the shameless inhumanity, the urge to degrade humankind physically and mentally through the threat of violence – is more deeply concerned with the minds that can reach such levels of depravity. This still leaves out of account the several characters in the play, Vittoria for one, who are lured into evil and through perpetrating it discover not only moral but social awareness. Vittoria comes to know her world more thoroughly than her brother, the satirist. Long before her death she has come to despise what initially she most coveted in the way of social 'preferment'. That process of disillusionment is balanced by a growing perception of her intrinsic merits. Preoccupied as he was with surface effect, Dunlop failed to reach Webster's challenging thesis. Consequently the production tended to support those critics who see *The White Devil* as a lurid melodrama relieved by moments of fine verse. The true poetic density of the play went largely unrealised.

9   MICHAEL LINDSAY-HOGG'S PRODUCTION OF *THE WHITE DEVIL* 1976

Glenda Jackson is renowned for her strong, even rather formidable stage personality. Adverse critics talk of it as a bored sultriness, the mark of one who is beyond surprise or a spontaneous gesture; to those admiring histrionic display her technique appears too contained. To her admirers the situation is quite different. Tutored by Peter Brook, she has learned to refine her style to an absolute economy of means. Her body is poised but has great flexibility of movement so that the smallest gesture *tells*; and these gestures move less to the rhythm of her speech than to the rhythm of her mind in its thinking. The role of Vittoria is difficult in that she appears in only five out of sixteen scenes and is seen passing over the stage in a procession in another; at each appearance the plot has advanced considerably and Vittoria's fortunes have changed in consequence. An actress has to structure the role's development without being present on stage regularly to chart the character's transitions (the part of Lady Macbeth poses a similar challenge). From the initial seduction to her trial, from her imprisonment in the House of Convertites to Brachiano's death and finally to her death scene, the part involves great emotional leaps. The play continually creates the contexts for her appearances, for Vittoria is either the cause of the action or the subject, directly or indirectly, of the dialogue; but the actress on reappearing has to imply the character's growth. It was here that Glenda Jackson's technique was at an advantage: you could sense her mind outstripping Monticelso's at the trial, for example, and grimly apprehending its inevitable conclusion long before the Cardinal actually succumbed to malice; from the moment she saw him she had the measure of his mind and knew herself powerless before its intrinsic chauvinism. Bored and sultry she may have been when we first encountered her but Vittoria was then trapped in a marriage of convenience that gave her life no meaning. It was the frustration of a great capacity to love and to live life to the full that Glenda Jackson saw as initiating Vittoria's tragedy: in a bleak existence she had the capacity to see life's richer potential and dared to try to seize hold of it. She was bored to the depths of her soul being dutifully submissive to a pedantic ass like Camillo. We could gauge the extent of her emotional and spiritual drudgery from the alacrity with which she responded to Flamineo's temptations and the fearful restraint with which she met Brachiano's approaches, as if dreading that present circumstance should repeat itself in yet another relationship. Jackson's Vittoria was a woman who had learned that woman's lot in life was largely to suffer, relieved only by the delight of giving pleasure to men rather than receiving it from them; she was a sophisticated beauty who smouldered with resentment at the indignity, the insult to her essential womanliness that that implied. Her trial was less a questioning of her moral worth than an arraignment of her by the leaders of the Church and State for being no more but e'en a woman, yet one having the temerity to claim the right to shape her own destiny. When she flinched with her whole body against Monticelso's abuse of the legal process, it was out of shocked recognition of his hatred of her sex; and when she majestically stood her ground, calmly showing him the degree to which he traduced his office as judge, she was defending more than her own self.

It might be objected that this was too 'feminist' and anachronistic an interpretation of the play made possible by the modern setting. Yet one never felt, as with Frank Dunlop's production, that the director's hand was intrusive; rather the text was allowed in a wholly unforced way to speak for itself. That the play had considerably modern social and psychological resonances enabled the audience quickly to pass beyond the dimension of plot and engage with Webster's subtext. This gave the play a deepening intensity, quite absent from Dunlop's version. The cold fury of Jackson's handling of the trial scene was in marked contrast to her appearance in the House of Convertites. Brachiano's presence at the trial, a gesture of seigniorial disdain in the battle of wills between the Duke and Francisco, had needlessly compromised Vittoria in order to flatter his *amour-propre*. When they are next together it is he, spurred on by Francisco's letter, who has the audacity to question her integrity. For Jackson's Vittoria this was a moment of terrible crisis: she met Brachiano in a rush of ardour but was reduced to abject humility by his accusations; her superior mind, once she saw the letter, immediately guessed at Francisco's trick and its objective; but to Brachiano, petulant with jealousy, his male pride challenged, her cleverness was downright impudence. She saw that to save the situation she had to flatter his sexual ego and provoke his appetite, but she did so with cynical disgust, apprehending in this how few of her initial hopes for the relationship with Brachiano had been realised. She now knew how right her presentiment had been at their first meeting; but she had lacked then enough experience to trust her intuitions. Now that she had learned to recognise and value her intelligence, all it could teach her was the extent of its betrayal by herself and others.

It was a world-weary Vittoria we discovered in the final act: married and widowed almost in an instant, still spiritually and emotionally hungry for fulfilment and despising herself for still knowing that need. The subtext that the production had established throughout the earlier acts of the play gave a terrible credibility of motivation to the violence of the last scene. When, after the shooting of the pistols in the suicide pact, Flamineo lay as if dead, Vittoria was impelled by a long-pent-up savagery to attack his 'corpse'. The text demands that she and Zanche trample on the body in triumphant delight; here it was a moment of ecstatic brutality as the once-elegant Vittoria abandoned herself to the luxury of sheer naked hatred against her brother, partly as the instigator of her spiritual decline but more crucially as the embodiment of all things male that she had come to loathe. The violence was both an expression and a purging of her self-pity, which left in her a strange calm to meet her death. The sequence for all its horror gave a profound motivation for Flamineo's total reappraisal of his sister as they lay dying. His transformation finely contrasted with Lodovico, who, finally getting his hands on the prey he has coveted from the very start of the play (for Vittoria 'might have got my pardon / For one kiss to the Duke' but did not), unleashed on her all his revulsion for her sex. Lifting her skirt with his sword, he stabbed her repeatedly in the groin. It was a hideous death yet of a piece with Vittoria's treatment throughout the play at the hands of men. Lodovico did physically what others perpetrated by subtler symbolic but equally perverse ways, even those who claimed to 'love' her. Jackson's was a superb characterisation, meticulously structured in its psychological progressions and at every stage integrated with Webster's text.

It was a fine stroke of imagination, given the modern setting of the revival, to cast James Villiers as Brachiano. He has made a reputation for himself in upper-class comedies as the embodiment of the English gentleman: courteous, assured, slightly stuffy (not to say pompous) at times, amiable, but breezily deficient in sensitivity. His light, briskly efficient touch in dismissing Isabella (Frances de la Tour) from his affections was the more unpleasant for his being quite oblivious of his cruelty; what was a heart-piercing tragedy to her was to him a convenient arrangement leaving his philandering nature a comfortably free rein. The scene was an ominous preparation for Brachiano's relationship with Vittoria, given her quest for emotional security; and this is indicative of how creatively Lindsay-Hogg responded to the patterns of parallels and contrasts with which Webster structures the tragedy.

Another notable piece of casting was Patrick Magee as Monticelso: his gravelly voice, mellowing at times into almost musical intoning, nicely caught the politician who shamelessly uses unctuous priestly rhetoric to command authority. But he could not long sustain his self-satisfied air in the presence of Vittoria's shrewd and undeviating stance and the voice thinned out to an insistent whine, while the nastiness of his threats merely showed how penetrating her appraisal of him had been. Sitting in judgement, he had been judged and he struggled to cover his spiritual nakedness but had nothing but spite left to him that Vittoria had not shown to be a sham; malice was his very essence.

Jonathan Pryce made Lodovico a study of an individual in whom slights are stored from time immemorial, steadily building up psychic tension that finds release in unparalleled atrocity. From the first his threats against Vittoria and Flamineo had unexpected menace; in his mind's eye he was already visualising for them different modes of death to find the fittest. This gave great weight to his observation when plotting Brachiano's end with Francisco:

> I would have our plot be ingenious,
> And have it hereafter recorded for example
> Rather than borrow example.
>
> [v i 75–7]

As the play advanced, despite his sober-suited appearance, he grew into a monster of depravity, his imagination focused wholly on the instinct for revenge. At the end of the play Edward Bond, who prepared the acting version for Lindsay-Hogg, made his only substantial adaptation of the text and did this seemingly to complete the portrait of Lodovico incisively. Hard on Flamineo's death, the young prince and his soldiers were heard arriving but could not enter, as Lodovico and Gasparo had barricaded themselves into the room with their victims. The soldiers began to hack down the obstruction while the final speeches were shouted incoherently offstage; in the mayhem Lodovico was shot by a machine gun in the spine (the only use of a modern weapon). Instantly silence fell and the last words heard were Lodovico's; he was not, like Vittoria and Flamineo, reaching for some judgement of his existence but, dragging himself over and over his victims' corpses he gloated in an ambition perfectly accomplished: 'here's my rest: / *I limb'd this night-piece and it was my best*' [v vi 294–5]. He was too satiated with the kill for the fact of his own death to impinge on his consciousness.

Sadly the one miscasting in the production was Jack Shepherd who approached the role of Flamineo in a characteristically downbeat style of understatement which, while it was in tune with the prevailing style of the production, went quite against the demands of the role. Where Jackson, Villiers, Magee and Pryce matched their personal techniques imaginatively to the demands of the play, Shepherd seemed at a loss for an appropriate style. His voice was too light, thin and lacking in tonal variety to capture Flamineo's shifts of mood. The unpleasant sides of the character were there – the shifty, menial mentality, the sickening voyeurism, the pander, the toady – but there was none of the energy, the preparedness for any eventuality that makes Flamineo dramatically exciting, and more crucially lacking were the thoughtless impetuosity that makes him the architect of his own downfall and the relish in being the actor that accompanies all his scheming. If that last quality is missing then his dying speeches, for all their poetic brilliance, lack dramatic point and seem like so much empty rhetoric, barely distinct from his satire of a dying actor in the mock suicide earlier in the scene. Flamineo's dynamism gives *The White Devil* much of its dramatic momentum; as a consequence of Shepherd's manner of playing, the role seemed to have simply that function of propelling the action forward. Paradoxically what is Webster's most complex characterisation in the play carried little impact as a psychological study beside the performances of the roles of

Brachiano and Lodovico, which are simpler in conception but open with sensitive playing to a richness of detail. In his final recognition of Vittoria's worth Shepherd achieved a new tone of rapt awe, yet the effect would have been still more moving if previously his role had encompassed a range of false tones by which we might have gauged more precisely his sudden access to sincerity. Shepherd's shortcomings or plain misreading of his role only served to throw into sharper focus Glenda Jackson's achievement for the full-blooded creation it was, because she inhabited the text, responsive always to the dramatic possibilities of the poetry. Lindsay-Hogg's was an excellent production, largely misprized – because mis-understood – by reviewers. We still await a production that does proper justice to that difficult role of Flamineo, a type so very much of its period in the tradition of the malcontent/fantastic that it demands a virtuoso range acompanied by great sensitivity in ensemble work (as challenging a role to play today as Lucio in *Measure for Measure*). Till then we shall be in want of a production that does justice to Webster's skilful structure of a double tragedy that explores the parallel career of brother and sister till, united in death, they discover a true consanguinity.

10   PETER GILL'S PRODUCTION OF *THE DUCHESS OF MALFI*, 1971

Prior to his production of *The Duchess of Malfi* Peter Gill had established himself at the Royal Court with a series of D. H. Lawrence's plays about Nottingham mining families – delicate, naturalistic studies of emotional tensions in households where few are gifted with the ability to analyse or express their feelings. The most lasting memory of his production of the Webster was his similar concern to explore it as a *domestic* tragedy. This was not to ignore the political aspects but to show politics as the destructive force in what should be lasting bonds of love and kinship between wife and husband, sister and brothers. There was a sense too of private, intimate worlds cruelly being exposed to public view. This was particularly the case with the Duchess and Antonio (played by Judy Parfitt and Desmond Gill): the scenes between them were full of a tender gaiety. In the wooing scene of Act I there was clearly already a relaxed atmosphere of trust between mistress and servant that relaxed even further from the formal, at first hesitantly as each tested the other's feelings to be sure of a mutual accord, before together they entered a state of quiet wonder. There was no intense passion at first, only a great stillness which defined the momentous social step they were taking in finding a new relation through marriage. The rapture here was wholly different in quality from the easy harmony in III ii, soon to be set at hazard by Ferdinand, where the tone intimated the comfort of a couple who now knew each other thoroughly and were blissfully content as each day renewed the pleasure of their companionship. Their parting at Ancona in consequence was deeply affecting with the Duchess arguing for what seemed best to secure for Antonio and his heir their political safety yet feeling uncertain about the wisdom of this decision after her drastic recent misjudgement of Bosola's trustworthiness which had reduced them all to this state of desperation. It was because Parfitt chose to play the two lovemaking scenes (as had Peggy Ashcroft in Donald McWhinnie's 1961 production at Stratford and the Aldwych) with a delicate ease and grace of wit that the panic of the preparations for Ancona became so ominous and the separation of the lovers so tragic yet inevitable a development. This was a production in which character determined the movement of the plot largely because the better actors like Parfitt and Gill were responsive to the varied rhythms of Webster's verse as his means of defining tone in specific scenes. There was a wealth of difference between their mischievous toying with classical allusions in the bedroom scene [III ii], suggestive of cultured minds at play, and their handling of conceits after the banishment [III v] like the dream of the Duchess's crown, where ideas, tersely expressed, punctured the silence like sharp stabs of pain, as the rhythm fragmented the verse lines into short, uneven units. This sensitivity to the fluctuations in each other's emotional moods ensured a complex pathos in their playing of the echo scene [v iii]. Staged with great simplicity (Parfitt as the echo was concealed within a tight cluster of actors standing in dim light with their backs to Antonio and Delio), the scene moved immediately from a 'real' to a psychological dimension: it was as if in the deep of the mind Antonio still heard his wife's voice as intuitions, but fear and despair so preoccupied his thoughts that he no longer dared trust such insights enough to act on them. The separation of this husband and wife was more than a physical and social fact; it was a divorce of sensibilities once marvellously attuned. What impressed about Peter Gill's direction was his sensitivity to this psychological structuring of the play; significantly too by working intensively with his actors on that level, Gill effortlessly made the basic story line of the tragedy crystal clear.

One consequence of highlighting the intimate family relationships of the play was the emergence of a theme not perhaps readily perceived from a reading of the text: the extent to which the characters will into being what they most fear. There was a desperate urgency about Ferdinand's advice to the Duchess that in her widowhood she live a demure, withdrawn existence, abjuring from her palace the excitements of feasts and masques; about his hiring of Bosola to spy on his sister and report whether she followed his instructions to the letter; about his anxious waiting for news from Malfi as if certain that his worst fears would be realised, his authority over her be flouted and he be impelled to act against her out of 'justice'. Yet in the darker reaches of his mind, he was already planning his terrible revenge almost before she had transgressed his imposed order. That finally he went mad was in sheer revulsion from the hideous self that emerged to confront him during the process of that revenge; the sequence of tortures in Act IV held a mirror up to his own nature too harrowing for him to accept and insanity was his only escape.

For Bosola there was the fear of generosity, of love and forgiveness, of altruistic qualities of the spirit that would challenge his belief in a pragmatic world where evil is the prevailing human condition and the power to inflict evil one's only resource. And yet, as Antonio senses from the first, there is the potential for good in Bosola, however rigorously he may try to suppress it. As the time of the Duchess's death approaches, Bosola refuses to go to her *in his own person* [IV i 131], as if he dimly apprehends some imminent personal cataclysm. But no superficial disguise can protect him: faced with the manner of her dying, he loses all self-possession and ends the play in a moral chaos precipitated by the emergence of a conscience that he has no power to direct.

For the Duchess and Antonio there was always the fear of discovery and reprisal that is the obverse of the courage they find together secretly to break with social and political convention; and this went a long way to justify their passivity in the face of disaster and Antonio's strange temper in Act v where fatalism takes on a mask of utterly naive optimism once he is deprived of the sure foundation the Duchess brings his life. There is no chance of the Cardinal's relenting and at heart he knows it.

For the Cardinal there was always the fear that his own devious nature would be made public, compromising his position as a prince of the Church. It was obviously a welcome relief to him to offload the tiresome Bosola on to Ferdinand in the opening act. His moral exhortations to his brother to control his anger [II v 47ff.] seemed motivated less by Christian concern than a cunning expediency lest Ferdinand should act in a way to confirm what at present are to the world at large but rumours, idle gossip about the Duchess's loose conduct and thereby implicate the whole family in scandal. When called upon to act on discovering the truth about the Duchess and Antonio, his way was not private and insidious like Ferdinand's but a careful, public demonstration of moral outrage at Ancona, a ritual and impersonal casting off of all family ties and responsibilities made in the full splendour of a religious ceremonial. When Julia's tactlessness with Bosola threatened to expose his real nature despite his cleverness at keeping his public image spotless, cool murder was his inevitable resource. But circumstance in the final carnage compelled him to admit to the sordid reality that was his life and hope that, dead, he would be 'laid by, and never thought of' [v v 90] and not be an object of infamy and derision.

While the production achieved overall this sense of patterning, it has to be admitted that not all the performances were as finely sustained as Judy Parfitt's and Desmond Gill's; the powerful emotional truth of their scenes together became very much the centre of the play with the effect of making the rest seem like a slowly encroaching nightmare, enveloping and extinguishing all but the Duchess's chastened spirit. The nightmare quality was further enhanced by the continual presence on stage of the chorus of actors not otherwise engaged in the scene. Paradoxically it emphasised the exceptional loneliness of the characters as their souls travelled this benighted progress, because of their continuing fear of someone discovering their secret inner selves. The chorus were that fear embodied, hovering always on the periphery of consciousness. It was a highly imaginative conception to make the essentials of the production-method yet again stress the psychological dimensions of Webster's tragedy: everything devised by Peter Gill carried an audience to an imaginative engagement with the play's subtexts. Perhaps only in the intimate confines of a theatre like the Royal Court could such a focus be directed at the intimacy within the play (it does make actors particularly vulnerable and not all of Peter Gill's cast could stand up to such rigorous scrutiny of their technique), but it proved the key to unlock the many dimensions of meaning *The Duchess of Malfi* contains within its structure. The austerity of the directorial method induced in the audience a profound richness of perception. The play performed became total metaphor.

11   PHILIP PROWSE'S PRODUCTION OF *THE DUCHESS OF MALFI*, 1985

Peter Gill's production of *The Duchess of Malfi* was perhaps finer in the conception than always in the execution because he was working with a young cast, many of whom were inexperienced in playing Renaissance verse drama; but, interestingly, that conception was strong enough to impress itself on a responsive audience despite the evident limitations of some of the actors. On paper Philip Prowse at the National Theatre had what promised to be an ideal cast: Ian McKellen (Bosola), Edward Petherbridge (the Cardinal), Jonathan Hyde (Ferdinand),

Eleanor Bron (the Duchess), Greg Hicks (Antonio), Selina Cadell (Cariola). All possess distinctive individual styles yet are accomplished ensemble actors. In the event they were none of them freed into their own creativity with the text but imprisoned within Prowse's elaborate visual schemes.

All too frequently visual imagery replaced Webster's verbal or structural patterning but to no immediately evident purpose. The Duchess and Ferdinand are twins; throughout the production their dress was always complementary: black for the first three acts, white for the final two; in the bedroom scene [III ii] where she was wearing a loose-fitting gown, he appeared to her equally unbraced in a black robe; throughout the torture sequences, she wore a white penitential garment and he likewise, though his was of coarser fabric. Whatever the psychological point was behind this – and much could have been made of it to define the relationship between the characters – it was not clarified by being pointedly related by director or actors to the text.

Dying, Bosola cries out against 'this gloomy world'; it is, he says, 'a shadow or deep pit of darkness' [v v 100–1]. This seemed very much to have inspired Prowse and his lighting designer, who deployed an array of unusually angled spotlights, many positioned at the level of the actors' feet, to throw phantasmagoric shadows looming over the walls of the setting. While Death literally walked amongst the characters, so each character's personal death seemed to hover over him or stalk his presence. This made for some telling theatrical images especially at the moment of the characters' actual deaths. The Duchess's strangling by Bosola and two black-cowled attendants was in technical terms simply done but by virtue of the ground-level lighting the stage seemed filled with giant, swirling, faceless shapes about her gaunt, isolated white figure. Similarly the final crescendo of deaths was frightening for being indistinct – a whirling, confused mass of violent gestures magnified over the setting that left a suddenly still, bleeding, diminutively life-sized heap of corpses caught in a stray shaft of light. These were powerful moments, fraught with an awesome tension. But it is crucially important that we actually focus on the characters' death speeches; in this instance the prevailing gloom and a uniform mode of delivering the lines that aimed at a breathless, pain-racked realism made it unclear which character was speaking at any given time so that Webster's fascination with how in death each character's consciousness sits in judgement on his existence was (quite literally) lost sight of amidst the frantic confusion.

Earlier in the tragedy the eerie lighting effects often threw the actors' faces into whole or partial shadow so that the play of the eyes and the facial muscles in conjunction with the spoken word, which is the actor's way of intimating a subtext of significance, proved impossible to achieve. Bosola with his soliloquies was most regularly the victim of this situation and Ferdinand in his degeneration into madness. The scene for these two characters immediately after the Duchess's death, which shows the Duke's consciousness reeling hellwards with a terrifying alacrity and his henchman's fearfully perceiving a way to spiritual ease to which his past life may deny him access, utterly lacked pathos for want of stillness and visual clarity, since Prowse set the characters circling each other and the Duchess's coffin in what seemed an ever-deepening darkness.

When Prowse perceived tonal and emotional complexity in the text, he tended again to try and realise it in visual terms: the Duchess by finding a point of stillness within transcends the horror of her murder, dispelling any fear that might reduce her mind to a state of despair; the token of this is her concern for the spiritual welfare of her executioners, the well-being of Cariola and her children, and her brothers' future ease. Though the tension steadily mounts, she dictates the calm pace of the event transforming it into a kind of ritual. As Prowse had previously cut all references to the children, some of the most famous lines in the play of necessity had to be excised here, inevitably affecting the tone and Webster's carefully calculated *tempo* at this point. Given the darkness and the increasingly menacing movement in the play of shadows about her, the actress in order to be in control of the proceedings had to resort to a voice of command, a hortatory shrillness at odds with the deeper significance of the event. Her murder involved a sustained guttural rattle cut short by the audible breaking of the neck bone. Sensational realism prevailed where Webster clearly envisaged a more stylised mode of performance that would allow the complexities of the moment to impinge fully on the audience's awareness. (Much more successful were the totally silent deaths of Peter Gill's production accompanied by mimed gestures expressive of intense pain, which allowed the audience to register the fact of the deaths while concentrating on Webster's evocation in the poetry of the various ways consciousness encounters the process of death.) As if seeking to restore some of Webster's complexity to the scene Prowse had his figure of Death cease pacing the perimeter of the action and, lying downstage of the coffin, ease the Duchess's corpse into it with a wide-armed gesture suggestive at once of welcome and exultation. The merely visual could not, however, compensate for the richness of Webster's artistry.

One visual effect of the production was the subject of intense critical debate: Prowse's decision to keep the Duchess on stage as a visible presence throughout the last act, her penitential robe replaced by a shining diaphanous gown. Side by side with Death, she was a ghostly witness of the action. John Barber of *The Daily Telegraph* considered this a directorial quirk in exceptionally poor taste; Emrys Jones in *The Times Literary Supplement* thought that in consequence 'the play's final movement becomes immeasurably strengthened'; Michael Billington in *The Guardian* argued that this was a misconception of Webster's nihilistic philosophy, that death is not for him a bourne from which travellers return, and Prowse was putting 'image before meaning'. Through two surreal episodes – the Duchess's partial reawakening in the coffin and the echo scene – Webster does intimate for her the possibility of resurrection; at no point in her dying does she see death as the black void feared by so many of Webster's characters. In some ways the image of the Duchess's continuing presence was further compensation for failing to stage the death scene with a proper sensitivity to the implications of the text. Beyond that, the image had its strengths and its weaknesses. The echo scene was one of the few times the production achieved a convincing pathos with a visible Duchess, her voice dispassionate and remote, striving to guide Antonio to his safety yet powerless actively to affect him. Because of this Antonio's death (so easily made to seem perfunctory in performance) was equally affecting, since with Death the Duchess appeared before him and his last breath brought him to her feet reaching up to her welcoming embrace. The tragic intensity of their playing in the echo scene saved this moment from sentimentality. More troubling, however, was the Duchess's calm watching of death being dealt her enemies, when the text of her own death scene absolves her of any impulse towards revenge. At this point the device created more philosophical problems than it resolved. The experiment was interesting but largely proved that it is preferable for a director to trust Webster's judgement.

One is tempted to add too on the strength of this production that it is preferable for a director to respect his actors. The setting was capaciously vast, using almost the full depth of the Lyttleton stage; after the initial processional sequence only the Duchess's death was played downstage; most of the action was played firmly back within the proscenium. This worked well at times for big cast scenes as when Antonio and Delio stand apart, watching and commenting on the crowd of sycophantic courtiers jostling for Ferdinand's attention. However most of the nineteen scenes involve only two or three characters on stage together; and it was a wanton disregard of the actors to place these scenes way back in the recesses of the set. For a start it risked audibility, for the setting given its cavernous dimensions was fraught with acoustic hazards; more importantly, it risked losing emotional subtlety (in, for example, the intimate scenes between the Duchess and Antonio) and nervous tension. This last point was especially the case in scenes like the 'apricot' episode [II i] where Bosola is scrutinising the Duchess's every move and intonation in the hope that she will betray herself. If the audience is not kept alert with apprehension here then Antonio's moments of privacy with the Duchess will not seem the haven of rest, the freedom from rigorous self-control that they should appear, nor will the Duchess's sudden reckless trust of Bosola in the course of preparing her flight to Ancona be felt to be the catastrophic gesture it is. Webster's dramatic method is cumulative, as this shows, and always in respect of tonal detail. But for that method to have its proper impact, an audience must be attentive to the actors and in the closest proximity to them. (In fairness to Philip Prowse, it must be admitted that his methods succeed better in the closer confines of the Glasgow Citizens' Theatre, his home base, though his recent production of

Racine's *Phèdre* for Glenda Jackson involved a setting that evoked a grandeur of scale while placing the actors right downstage.)

The consequence of the production-method chosen for *The Duchess of Malfi* was a series of performances from the actors that seemed at best only two-dimensional. Eleanor Bron's Duchess was from the first mature with greying hair and heavy-lidded eyes; her wooing of Antonio was a last desperate grasp at youth and infatuation; she seemed ever apprehensive of coming doom, so there was no space in her reading of the role for the gaiety and wit Ashcroft and Parfitt found in the early acts. The audience must sense a deliberate contrast between the Duchess's wooing of Antonio's love in Act I and Julia's predatory assault on Bosola's lust in Act V; it is part of the moral strategy of the play; but Eleanor Bron's love scenes were too tense, too anxious for gratification, for this structural patterning to work. McKellen too was disappointing as Bosola: he caught the initial complexity of the role – the soured intellectual compelled by circumstance and ill-luck to be the instrument of others' evil; the corrosive disgust with the world, the flesh and himself. But he quite missed the development of the character when conscience begins to permeate his awareness, undermine his assurance and lead him into an agony of doubt and moral uncertainty. Unfortunate cutting of his part left it unclear why he had decided to support Antonio against the Cardinal and why this was a tragic misapplying of his new-found conscience. The performance failed as a result to invest Bosola with tragic dignity. Jonathan Hyde as Ferdinand played almost throughout at a pitch of rage so again there was no sense of development in the role, of the madman deep suppressed within his nature that relentlessly surfaces to take total possession of his being. It was interesting that Hyde and Prowse chose to present the madness visually not in terms of the wolf-man of Webster's text but rather in terms of a demented religious zealot, half-naked but for a wrap of grubby sackcloth and wielding a sword like some rough crook or crucifix. Throughout in his own mind Ferdinand believes he is acting out of justice; there was therefore some ironic point to Hyde's chosen appearance as a zany prophet, but it was an idea that needed preparation in the early acts of the play, if its symbolic potential was to be at all clear. The performers who did make an impact were those in the smaller cameo-roles like Sheila Hancock as Julia (turning up secretly in the Cardinal's appartment to surprise him clad in leather boots and doublet like a strapping, cheeky squire), where the text leaves room for a broader style of acting that could build effects on Prowse's visual imagery.

The problems with this production were all ultimately the result of Prowse's refusal to let Webster's verse inhabit the foreground of the actors' and the audiences' imaginations. By trying visually to realise the atmosphere of the play he drastically simplified or undermined Webster's meaning and, most seriously for a tragedy, robbed the action of Webster's compassionate concern with the intricate, enigmatic impulses that shape his characters' moral natures. For all its monumental splendours, the production lacked any feeling for human dignity. That is to traduce Webster's art and vision.

12   CONCLUSION

The pictorial approach to Renaissance tragedy will work, it seems, no better for Webster than for Shakespeare. On the evidence of these four productions a preferable method appears to be to allow the packed verse to make its dramatic impact within a production that is sensitive to Webster's deep preoccupation with character and his creation of a dramatic structure that, through various devices of patterning with scenes, encourages an audience to make ever subtler moral discriminations about the society his plays portray. Webster is fascinated by the ways conscience manifests itself in the psyche and the ways minds free themselves from the burden of guilt. This is not to argue that he is an aridly moralistic dramatist. He also delights in the arts of the theatre – acting, mime, music, spectacle – and exploits them richly, but to a distinctive purpose. Always his concern is to make his stage-action a metaphor for the inner lives of his characters. Those

productions have succeeded best which have placed their main
focus on emotional and moral realism rather than on realism of
sensational effect in violence and spectacle. Usually it is the
production that severely stylises its surface effects that releases
an audience imaginatively into a full appraisal of the interplay
of character beyond its immediate significance for the
development of the plot. Webster is perhaps our most
completely metaphysical dramatist and that in a far wider
sense than is implied by T. S. Eliot's line about the dramatist's
ability to see 'the skull beneath the skin' (a view that too
strongly coloured Philip Prowse's conception of *The Duchess of
Malfi*). Webster could discern the spirit too, the inner
dimension of self that keeps pace with a character's progress
through the physical realities of the plot and that finally in
death gains total possession of the character's consciousness.
The challenge for a director and cast is to keep an audience
attuned to that other dimension of being which is best achieved
by exploring the dramatic possibilities of the verse. Significantly
productions remarkable for their economy, restraint and
discipline have come closest to realising the dense texture of
implication in the tragedies. There is no such thing as the
definitive production; but the modern theatre has yet to do
Webster's genius full justice.

READING LIST

EDITIONS

The edition used throughout has been that by David Gunby in *John Webster: Three Plays* published in the Penguin English Library in 1972. This contains a sound introduction to the two tragedies, notes on sources and a detailed analysis of each play's dramatic structure. Other fine editions are those by John Russell Brown for The Revels Plays (*The White Devil*, 1960 and *The Duchess of Malfi*, 1964) and by Elizabeth Brennan for the New Mermaid Series (*The White Devil*, 1966 and *The Duchess of Malfi*, 1964). John Russell Brown's edition of *The Duchess of Malfi* includes the text of Webster's source for the play from Painter's *The Palace of Pleasure*.

CRITICAL ESSAYS AND STUDIES

Webster: The Critical Heritage, edited by Don D. Moore (1981), contains the texts of much of the critical material cited in my Introduction to Part One and valuable accounts of eighteenth and nineteenth-century adaptations and stagings of Webster's tragedies. The Macmillan Casebook on the plays, edited by R. V. Holdsworth (1975), gives a fuller account of twentieth-century developments in the criticism of Webster's art and includes reviews of productions from 1919 to 1971. For a valuable study of the social and political background of the plays I would recommend Lisa Jardine's *Still Harping on Daughters: Women and Drama in the Age of Shakespeare* (Brighton, 1983). An exhaustive study of Webster's source materials can be found in Gunnar Boklund's *The Sources of "The White Devil"* (Uppsala, 1957) and *"The Duchess of Malfi": Sources, Themes, Characters* (Harvard, 1962). M. C. Bradbrook's *Themes and Conventions of Elizabethan Tragedy* (Cambridge, 1935) and her *John Webster: Citizen and Dramatist* (London, 1980) set Webster's

plays firmly in the theatrical history of their time, while
Inga-Stina Ekeblad's 'The Impure Art of John Webster' in the
Review of English Studies (IX, 1958, pp. 253–67) offers a detailed
exploration of his debts to the tradition of the masque and his
fascination with theatrical effect. In the Mermaid Critical
Commentaries, *John Webster*, edited by Brian Morris (London,
1970), contains a range of fine essays on the problems of the
plays in performance, Webster's control of audience-response,
his realism and his use of tragicomedy. Emrys Jones
contributed a stimulating review of Philip Prowse's production
of *The Duchess of Malfi* to the Commentary section of *The Times
Literary Supplement* on 19 July 1985.

INDEX OF NAMES